D0393777

CONDUCT UNBECOMING

Hyperactivity, Attention Deficit, and Disruptive Behavior Disorders

■ **Anorexia Nervosa:**
Starving for Attention

■ **Child Abuse and Neglect:**
Examining the Psychological Components

■ **Conduct Unbecoming:**
Hyperactivity, Attention Deficit, and Disruptive Behavior Disorders

■ **Cutting the Pain Away:**
Understanding Self-Mutilation

■ **Drowning Our Sorrows:**
Psychological Effects of Alcohol Abuse

■ **Life Out of Focus:**
Alzheimer's Disease and Related Disorders

■ **The Mental Effects of Heroin**

■ **Psychological Disorders Related to Designer Drugs**

■ **Psychological Effects of Cocaine and Crack Addiction**

■ **Schizophrenia:**
Losing Touch with Reality

■ **Sibling Rivalry:**
Relational Disorders Between Brothers and Sisters

■ **Smoke Screen:**
Psychological Disorders Related to Nicotine Use

■ **Through a Glass Darkly:**
The Psychological Effects of Marijuana and Hashish

■ **The Tortured Mind:**
The Many Faces of Manic Depression

■ **When Families Fail:**
Psychological Disorders Caused by Parent-Child Relational Problems

■ **A World Upside Down and Backwards:**
Reading and Learning Disorders

THE ENCYCLOPEDIA OF PSYCHOLOGICAL DISORDERS

Senior Consulting Editor Carol C. Nadelson, M.D.
Consulting Editor Claire E. Reinburg

CONDUCT UNBECOMING

Hyperactivity, Attention Deficit, and Disruptive Behavior Disorders

Elizabeth Russell Connelly

CHELSEA HOUSE PUBLISHERS
Philadelphia

The ENCYCLOPEDIA OF PSYCHOLOGICAL DISORDERS *provides up-to-date information on the history of, causes and effects of, and treatment and therapies for problems affecting the human mind. The titles in this series are not intended to take the place of the professional advice of a psychiatrist or mental health care professional.*

Chelsea House Publishers
Editor in Chief: Stephen Reginald
Managing Editor: James D. Gallagher
Production Manager: Pamela Loos
Art Director: Sara Davis
Picture Editor: Judy L. Hasday
Senior Production Editor: Lisa Chippendale

Staff for CONDUCT UNBECOMING
Editorial Assistant: Anne Hill
Picture Researcher: Sandy Jones
Associate Art Director: Takeshi Takahashi
Designer / Cover Design: Brian Wible

The ChelseaHouse World Wide Web site address is
http://www.chelseahouse.com

Library of Congress Cataloging-in-Publication Data

Connelly, Elizabeth Russell.
Attention deficit/hyperactivity disorder, and other disruptive
behavior disorders / Elizabeth Russell Connelly.
 p .cm. — (Encyclopedia of psychological disorders)
Includes bibliographical references and index.
Summary: Describes disruptive behavior disorders before going on
to discuss historical documentation of their appearance, their
causes, treatments, and impact on society.
ISBN 0-7910-4895-0 (hc)
1. Attention-deficit hyperactivity disorder—Juvenile literature.
2. Behavior disorders in children—Juvenile literature.
[1. Attention-deficit hyperactivity disorder.] I. Title.
II. Series.
RJ506.H9RC645 1998
618.92'8589—dc21   98-3756
                                                             CIP
  3 4 5 67 8 9 10   AC

CONTENTS

Introduction by Carol C. Nadelson, M.D.   6

Disruptive Behavior Disorders   9

1   What Are Disruptive Behavior Disorders?   11

2   History of Disruptive Behavior Disorders   21

3   What Is Attention Deficit/Hyperactivity Disorder?   27

4   Conduct Disorder and Oppositional Defiant Disorder   37

5   The Impact on Society   49

6   The Causes of Disruptive Behavior Disorders   57

7   Treating Attention Deficit/Hyperactivity Disorder   67

8   Treating Other Disruptive Behavior Disorders   83

Appendix : For More Information   90

Appendix : Famous People with Attention Deficit Disorder   91

Sources Cited   92

Further Reading   96

Glossary   98

Index   100

PSYCHOLOGICAL DISORDERS AND THEIR EFFECT

CAROL C. NADELSON, M.D.
PRESIDENT AND CHIEF EXECUTIVE OFFICER,
The American Psychiatric Press

There are a wide range of problems that are considered psychological disorders, including mental and emotional disorders, problems related to alcohol and drug abuse, and some diseases that cause both emotional and physical symptoms. Psychological disorders often begin in early childhood, but during adolescence we see a sharp increase in the number of people affected by these disorders. It has been estimated that about 20 percent of the U.S. population will have some form of mental disorder sometime during their lifetime. Some psychological disorders appear following severe stress or trauma. Others appear to occur more often in some families and may have a genetic or inherited component. Still other disorders do not seem to be connected to any cause we can yet identify. There has been a great deal of attention paid to learning about the causes and treatments of these disorders, and exciting new research has taught us a great deal in the last few decades.

The fact that many new and successful treatments are available makes it especially important that we reject old prejudices and outmoded ideas that consider mental disorders to be untreatable. If psychological problems are identified early, it is possible to prevent serious consequences. We should not keep these problems hidden or feel shame that we or a member of our family has a mental disorder. Some people believe that something they said or did caused a mental disorder. Some people think that these disorders are "only in your head" so that you could "snap out of it" if you made the effort. This type of thinking implies that a treatment is a matter of willpower or motivation. It is a terrible burden for someone who is suffering to be blamed for their misery, and often people with psychological disorders are not treated compassionately. We hope that the information in this book will teach you about various mental illnesses.

The problems covered in the volumes in the ENCYCLOPEDIA OF PSYCHOLOGICAL DISORDERS were selected because they are of particular importance to young adults, because they affect them directly or because they affect family and friends. There are individual volumes on reading disorders, attention deficit and disruptive behavior disorders, and dementia—all of these are related to our abilities to learn and integrate information from the world around us. There are books on drug abuse that provide useful information about the effects of these drugs and treatments that are available for those individuals who have drug problems. Some of the books concentrate on one of the most common mental disorders, depression. Others deal with eating disorders, which are dangerous illnesses that affect a large number of young adults, especially women.

Most of the public attention paid to these disorders arises from a particular incident involving a celebrity that awakens us to our own vulnerability to psychological problems. These incidents of celebrities or public figures revealing their own psychological problems can also enable us to think about what we can do to prevent and treat these types of problems.

Disruptive behavior disorders, usually first diagnosed in childhood, often have a negative impact on a child's relationships with family, teachers, and peers.

DISRUPTIVE BEHAVIOR DISORDERS:
AN OVERVIEW

*D*isruptive behavior disorder is a general term that the American Psychiatric Association uses to refer to several psychological conditions that are typically first diagnosed in childhood or adolescence: attention deficit/hyperactivity disorder (ADHD), conduct disorder, and oppositional defiant disorder. However, although these disorders are usually identified at an early age, their effects may extend well into adulthood.

Attention deficit/hyperactivity disorder is a developmental disorder of self-control. Children or adults with ADHD either have a problem with inattention, or are hyperactive and impulsive. Conduct disorder and oppositional defiant disorder, unlike ADHD, involve violations of others' rights, confrontations with adults or authority figures, and even violence in the most severe cases.

Disruptive behavior disorders can affect a child's education and relationships at home and with friends, and they can lead to trouble at home or work later in life. However, these disorders can be treated. People who have struggled with attention deficit/hyperactivity disorder or a related disorder include famous thinkers (Albert Einstein, Galileo Galilei, Leonardo da Vinci), artists (Wolfgang Amadeus Mozart, F. Scott Fitzgerald, George Bernard Shaw), entertainers (Walt Disney, John Lennon), and athletes (Greg Louganis, Pete Rose). With early diagnosis, a successful program of treatment, and support from family, teachers, and friends, children can overcome the effects of disruptive behavior disorders.

Children with attention deficit/hyperactivity disorder often find themselves avoided by peers and feel "stupid" because of difficulties with schoolwork. As a result, these children develop low self-esteem and feelings of despair.

1

WHAT ARE DISRUPTIVE BEHAVIOR DISORDERS?

B en was seven years old and in the first grade when he was first diagnosed with attention deficit/hyperactivity disorder (ADHD) and a learning disability.

Ben's parents had seen signs that their son was struggling with academics and social interactions when he was four years old. Pre-school screening revealed that his development was delayed in many areas, so Ben attended a special preschool for one year. After this, he went on to kindergarten and performed satisfactorily, but when Ben entered first grade his teacher noticed that he had difficulty paying attention to one task for more than a few minutes. This behavior frustrated his classmates, and they avoided him. At home, Ben's own frustration was evident, as he would say things like "I wish I was never born!" or "I'm stupid!"

Fortunately, Ben had an extremely patient first-grade teacher. His parents and teacher agreed that Ben should be evaluated for learning disabilities. During this evaluation, each time Ben tried and failed he would sink farther down into his seat. His self-esteem was taking a beating. At the end of the testing, however, the doctor told Ben that he wasn't dumb, but that his brain simply had a hard time keeping track of things. The doctor found that Ben tested positive for dyslexia and was below the first-grade level in reading and writing skills. Ben also had trouble repeating numbers dictated to him, normally a simple task.

The doctor speculated that Ben had ADHD but told his parents that there are no definitive tests to diagnose the syndrome. It is identified mainly by asking questions regarding behavior and progress at school. (Another doctor once compared having ADHD to a short in the wiring of a radio: Sometimes the radio produces the sounds it should and sometimes the connection just isn't there. Fix the connection and the radio works fine.)

When the doctor suggested treatment with methylphenidate (Ritalin), a drug that would enable the neurotransmitters in Ben's brain to make the right connections, his parents were relieved.

After Ben had been taking Ritalin for about a week his teacher reported that she saw a noticeable difference in his attention span and commitment to tasks. Other school staff and Ben's peers also noticed an improvement. Perhaps more important, Ben himself could tell a difference. Although he still struggled academically, partly because of his learning disability, he wasn't just that "dumb" kid in class anymore and he began to be included in after-school birthday parties and functions. This, in turn, helped his self-esteem even more.

Ben's struggle with attention-deficit disorder illustrates only one aspect of what the American Psychiatric Association (APA) terms disruptive behavior disorders. This umbrella term encompasses three psychological conditions that are typically first diagnosed in childhood or adolescence: attention deficit/hyperactivity disorder, conduct disorder, and oppositional defiant disorder. Some combination of the three is often present at the same time in the same individual. How they affect each individual varies, depending on the mix of factors that identify each disorder, the seriousness of those symptoms, and the persistence of behavioral patterns. Some youngsters may progress from oppositional defiant disorder to attention deficit/hyperactivity disorder or conduct disorder. But each case is different.

All three syndromes are usually associated with a degree of distress or disability. In somewhat simplistic terms, the more persistent the disorder, the greater the disability. However, although an individual is diagnosed with a particular disorder, he or she does not necessarily lack complete control over his or her behavior. Diminished control may be a feature of the disorder, but a diagnosis does not mean the person is (or was) unable to control his or her conduct at a particular time. It also must be noted that normal, culturally sanctioned responses to trauma—such as the death of a loved one—do not warrant a diagnosis even though some reactions may be similar to symptoms associated with these disorders. In order for a person to be diagnosed with attention deficit/hyperactivity disorder, conduct disorder, or oppositional defiant disorder, clear evidence of interference with developmentally appropriate social, academic, or occupational functioning must exist.

Attention deficit/hyperactivity disorder is fairly common in school-age children. Approximately 10 percent of boys and 2 percent of girls are diagnosed with the disorder.

ATTENTION DEFICIT/ HYPERACTIVITY DISORDER

Attention deficit/hyperactivity disorder was once considered simply a child's disorder indicated by a loose mix of annoying behaviors and scattered attention. Although ADHD is now understood to afflict people of all ages, most of the available research has concentrated on children and adolescents. Many documented findings about ADHD in children and adolescents have led to working hypotheses and specula-

Fighting is a common problem with children who have conduct disorder. This disruptive behavior disorder is characterized by repeated violations of other people's personal rights or of the rules of society.

tions about the same disorder in adults. So far, most of the findings regarding adults have been consistent with prior findings in youths with ADHD. Though attention deficit/hyperactivity disorder has multiple causes, it is related more to biological—neurological and genetic— factors than to purely social ones.

Approximately 10 percent of boys and 2 percent of girls have ADHD, so general prevalence is estimated at 3 to 5 percent of the school-age population in the United States. Unfortunately, accurate figures concerning the prevalence of ADHD in the adult population are limited.

Major symptoms of attention deficit/hyperactivity disorder (ADHD) include hyperactivity, impulsivity, and inattention. In the example earlier in the chapter, Ben's problem was predominantly inattention, and he also experienced the all-too-common secondary characteristic of emotional instability.

For ADHD to be diagnosed, some hyperactive-impulsive or inattentive symptoms that cause impairment must have been present before the child is seven years old, although many individuals are diagnosed after that age. In addition, a certain degree of impairment resulting from these symptoms must be present in at least two settings, such as at home and at school or work.

The intensity of symptoms varies across settings, depending on environmental structure, sensory stimulation, and emotional state, as well as on such physiological factors such as general alertness, hunger, and sleep deprivation. Most children experience more environmental pressure at school than at home, and the resultant hyperactivity and impulsive behavior is particularly clear in the classroom. Hyperactivity, impulsivity, and inattention are also increased in noisy places or group settings, such as hallways or crowded waiting rooms. The child may appear quite different to observers in different environments. For example, symptoms are often more apparent to the teacher in noisy or crowded settings than to the physician in a quiet office.

Attention-deficit/hyperactivity disorder is commonly seen in association with other psychiatric disorders, particularly conduct disorder, which is defined below. These coexisting disorders can appear independently, but they usually operate together, and have a common or shared cause. For example, ADHD is often seen with mood and anxiety disorders, typically with each disorder exacerbating the course of the other; but symptoms similar to those of ADHD can also occur as a result of the mood and anxiety disorders. These "ADHD look-alikes" may cause behavior that appears to be the result of ADHD or may occur in conjunction with ADHD. As a result, mistaken diagnoses are common. Attention deficit/hyperactivity disorder look-alikes can include conduct disorder, oppositional defiant disorder, major depressive disorder, bipolar disorder, post-traumatic stress disorder, and Tourette's syndrome.

Oppositional defiant disorder is characterized by a pattern of disobedience toward authority figures or adults. It is generally less serious than conduct disorder, and children with this disorder usually do not direct their anger toward their peers.

CONDUCT DISORDER

Conduct disorder is the most common behavioral diagnosis in child and adolescent patients in both clinic and hospital settings. Conduct disorder entails repeated violations of others' personal rights or of societal rules and includes violent and nonviolent behaviors. The syndrome is not a single medical entity, but a final common pathway for a variety of forms of misbehavior, ranging from frequent deception, running away, and truancy to serious crimes such as rape and armed robbery. Conduct disorder can derive from psychiatric disease, including mood disorders and psychosis, organic impairment and mental retardation, or personality disorders. Socioeconomic and environmental factors may also contribute heavily in many individuals.

Conduct disorder may occur as early as age 5 to 6 years but is usually diagnosed in late childhood or early adolescence. The onset of this disorder is rare after age 16. The course of conduct disorder varies, but early onset predicts an increased risk in adult life for antisocial personality disorder and substance abuse–related disorders. Although forms of the condition constitute some of the most severe behavioral disorders of childhood, only a fraction of affected children are treated. Many are rehabilitated, but some lead lives of delinquency or undergo long-term incarceration. Because of the possibility of such a severe outcome, the validity of a single categorical grouping has been questioned by proponents of a more dimensional approach to conduct problems. Thus the American Psychiatric Association has taken a step in that direction by dividing conduct disorder into two subgroups: childhood-onset and adolescent-onset.

Approximately 10 percent of the general child and adolescent population in the United States are estimated to have conduct disorder. And the prevalence of this disorder appears to have increased during the past two to three decades, and seems to occur more often in urban settings than in rural environments. Young men are more likely to suffer from conduct disorder. However, in recent years, the prevalence of conduct disorder has been increasing in young women and girls.

OPPOSITIONAL DEFIANT DISORDER

Oppositional defiant disorder is a distinct disruptive behavior disorder, one in which individuals exhibit difficult behavior that is not as severe as that seen in conduct disorder. Considerable research is still needed to define its cause and clinical characteristics as well as its prevalence in the general population and relationship to other disorders. The relatively few studies that have been completed indicate that oppositional defiant disorder does not have the same genetic transmission, psychological dynamics, family features, or drug responsiveness that are seen in psychosis or mood disorders; however, its causes are still uncertain.

The essential feature of oppositional defiant disorder is a recurrent pattern of negative, defiant, disobedient, and hostile behavior toward authority figures that persists for at least 6 months and is characterized by the frequent occurrence of at least four of the following behaviors:

- Actively defying or refusing to comply with the requests or rules of adults
- Throwing temper tantrums
- Arguing with adults
- Deliberately doing things that will annoy other people
- Swearing; using bad language
- Blaming others for his or her own mistakes or misbehavior
- Being touchy or easily annoyed by others
- Behaving in a spiteful or vindictive manner

Oppositional defiant disorder usually becomes evident before a child is eight years old. In males, the disorder has been shown to be more prevalent among those who, during their preschool years, have exhibited problematic temperaments such as extreme reactions or difficulty being soothed. It is also more prevalent in those who exhibited low self-esteem, severe mood swings, frustration, swearing, and use of alcohol, tobacco, or illicit drugs during the school years.

Children with oppositional defiant disorder show argumentative and disobedient behavior, but unlike children with conduct disorder, they respect the personal rights of other people. The oppositional and angry behavior demonstrated by these children does not lead to impulsive tendencies throughout their conduct, emotions, and thinking. The anger is typically directed at parents and teachers, and, to a lesser degree, may surface in relationships with friends and peers. Within families, there may be a vicious cycle in which the parent and child bring out the worst in each other. Oppositional defiant disorder is more prevalent in families in which child care is disrupted by a succession of different caregivers or in families in which harsh, inconsistent, or neglectful child-rearing practices are common.

Approximately 6 percent of children are estimated to have oppositional defiant disorder, with 75 percent of those male, according to one study (Anderson et al., 1987). After children reach puberty, the rates of occurrence for oppositional defiant disorder are approximately equal for males and females. Symptoms are generally similar in each sex, except that males may have more confrontational behavior and more persistent symptoms.

Attention deficit/hyperactivity disorder is common in children with oppositional defiant disorder. In a significant proportion of cases, oppositional defiant disorder precedes conduct disorder.

Disruptive behavior disorders like attention deficit/hyperactivity disorder are present in approximately five percent of the school-age children in the United States. Although the effects of disruptive behavior disorders have been documented throughout history, the conditions themselves were not studied until the early 20th century.

2

HISTORY OF DISRUPTIVE BEHAVIOR DISORDERS

O riginally described in antiquity and documented in anecdotes throughout world literature, attention-deficit/hyperactivity disorder was first identified on a large scale in the early 20th century, when children with von Economo's encephalitis, an inflammation of the brain, developed symptoms of hyperactivity, impulsivity, and inattention. After an epidemic of encephalitis that occurred in 1917, a link was established between adults who had developed abnormal behavioral conditions involving inattention from encephalitis and children with encephalitis who had symptoms of hyperactivity, inattention, and impulsive behavior. Two decades later, this link was strengthened by studies confirming the therapeutic effects of amphetamine on both conditions.

Amphetamine was the first non-barbiturate drug to be clinically effective in modern psychological treatment. It was developed in the late 1930s and studied in children with severe behavior disorders. These hyperactive, inattentive, and impulsive individuals had been labeled as having "minimal brain damage," even though there is no direct evidence of brain damage with this disorder; "minimal brain dysfunction," despite the fact that overt neurological damage produces similar dysfunction; and "hyperkinetic syndrome" and "hyperactivity syndrome," although other factors in addition to motor systems are involved. Today the term "attention deficit/hyperactivity disorder" more accurately defines the disorder.

The name and classification of ADHD have undergone a number of changes during the past several decades. In the 1960s the disorder was considered to be a "hyperkinetic reaction of childhood." In the 1970s, the American Psychiatric Association renamed the disorder attention deficit disorder (ADD) and emphasized inattention as its core feature. By the late 1980s, the disorder was reclassified as attention deficit/hyperactivity disorder (ADHD). Both inattention and hyperactivity were emphasized as equally important core features. The label attention deficit/hyperactivity disorder remains today, but three subtypes of ADHD are now recognized, depending on which symptoms prevail: a predominantly inattentive subtype, a predominantly hyperactive-impulsive subtype, and a combined subtype.

In the domain of child psychiatry, the much-diagnosed attention-deficit/hyperactivity disorder is an example of a condition that has progressed from observed behavior, to syndrome status, to perhaps an overly popularized disorder with widely prescribed pharmacological and behavioral treatments, to an accepted diagnosis for both children and adults. Fortunately, it is now less often diagnosed and more conservatively treated than it was in the 1970s and 1980s.

CONDUCT DISORDER

In the 1950s a number of doctors, inspired by early psychoanalyst Dr. August Aichhorn's studies of the behavioral causes of the "wayward youth" of Vienna two decades earlier, proposed a variety of ideas to help understand impulsive youngsters. One study in 1952 examined the adolescents' enactment of their parents' unconscious delinquent tendencies (Johnson and Szurek, 1952). Another study five years later described the failure of ego controls, leading to low self-esteem, underlying the difficulties of "children who hate" (Redl and Wineman, 1957). The next year, yet another study interpreted the "antisocial tendency" as an effort to test and secure relationships (Winnicott, 1958). Such contributions stirred up hope and therapeutic enthusiasm. Yet during the following three decades, enthusiasm gave way to widespread disillusionment and skepticism about the use of psychoanalysis in general and psychotherapy in particular for youths with conduct disorders.

Beginning in the early 1960s, other approaches attempted to address the questions that arose regarding youngsters with conduct disorder. Up until the late 1970s and early 1980s, sociocultural models (Cloward and Ohlin, 1960; Rutter and Giller, 1983) were the prevailing method of study. These models attempted to identify the significance of the following to the presentation of conduct disorder in an individual: socioeconomic class; family size; access to social, medical, and psychiatric services; child-rearing and socializing practices; and modes of exposure

Treatment of attention deficit/hyperactivity disorder and conduct disorder has improved because medical professionals are better able to diagnose the disorders than they were 20 years ago. However, conduct disorder may persist into adulthood despite therapy.

to alcohol and drugs. Around 1977, neurological models were being more widely applied to determine links with genetic influences, psychiatric vulnerabilities, attention-deficit/hyperactivity, learning disabilities, and depression (Christiansen, 1977; Lewis, 1983). Finally, family interaction models took over in the early 1980s and continue to be part of research efforts today. These models aid in determining the importance of parental violence and physical abuse, marital discord, and parental inadequacies in providing structure, supervision, and emotional involvement (Patterson, 1982; Patterson et al., 1992).

Despite efforts to treat conduct disorder that span nearly a century, the number of patients diagnosed with the syndrome appear to have increased over the last several decades. Today, approximately 10 percent of males and 6 percent of females in the United States suffer from conduct disorder, and the number of young women diagnosed with this problem is growing.

OPPOSITIONAL DEFIANT DISORDER

Compared to formally diagnosed attention-deficit/hyperactivity disorder and conduct disorder, oppositional defiant disorder is a relatively new concept. The characterization of this disorder has evolved from opposition to the requests or expectations of authority figures to a pat-

Traditionally, disruptive behavior disorders are first noticed in a school setting. When a child has trouble interacting with his or her peers, teachers will notify the child's parents. If the problem is severe, the child may be referred to a doctor for analysis.

tern of angry, aggressive, and negative behavior.

Oppositional behavior was first given serious consideration in the mid-1950s. Up until that time, there was little interest in the distinction between the normal defiant behavior seen in children, especially adolescents, and the persistent negativism and refusal to respect authority that was present in what was believed to be relatively few cases. Then, in 1955, Dr. Eugene Levy drew attention to this type of disruptive conduct, highlighting negativism as the core feature of oppositional behavior. A decade later, The Group for the Advancement of Psychiatry, in their 1966 report *Psychopathological Disorders in Childhood: Theoretical Considerations and a Proposed Classification*, elaborated on Dr. Levy's concept and established the label "oppositional personality disorder" to describe children who express aggressiveness through oppositional behavior.

By 1980, the American Psychiatric Association (APA) had formally categorized the syndrome as oppositional disorder, further refining the definition to include persistently disobedient, negative, and provocative opposition to authority figures. At the same time, the APA also introduced a list of five symptoms, at least two of which would have to be present for a child to be diagnosed with this disorder:

- disobeys or violates rules
- often loses temper
- is often argumentative
- provokes fights
- acts stubborn

Seven years later, the APA changed the name to oppositional defiant disorder and placed it, together with ADHD and conduct disorder, under the heading of disruptive behavior disorders. Additional warning signs (listed on page 18) were compiled by the APA to counter the prevailing criticism that oppositional disorder could not be distinguished from normal behavior.

The most recent, albeit minor, event in the history of this disorder occurred in 1994, when the APA reduced the minimum number of symptoms necessary for a diagnosis from five to four.

A child who has trouble paying attention to simple tasks may have the type of attention deficit/hyperactivity disorder that is characterized primarily by inattention. Another form of ADHD is characterized mainly by hyperactivity.

3

WHAT IS ATTENTION DEFICIT/HYPERACTIVITY DISORDER?

A ttention deficit/hyperactivity disorder is a developmental disorder of self-control. In a discussion of ADHD, Dr. Edward M. Hallowell, one of the nation's leading specialists in the disorder, tried to explain what life is like for children who suffer from attention deficit/hyperactivity disorder:

> What's it like to have ADD? Buzzing. Being here and there and everywhere. Someone once said, "Time is the thing that keeps everything from happening all at once." Time parcels moments out into separate bits so that we can do one thing at a time. In ADD, this does not happen. In ADD, time collapses. . . . To the person with ADD it feels as if everything is happening all at once. . . . The individual loses perspective and the ability to prioritize. He or she is always on the go, trying to keep the world from caving in on top.

According to the *Diagnostic and Statistical Manual of Mental Disorders,* fourth edition *(DSM-IV)*, children or adults with ADHD either have a problem with inattention, such as a short attention span or an inability to block out distractions, or are hyperactive and impulsive. One form of attention-deficit/hyperactivity disorder combines both of these symptoms.

There are no major physical characteristics associated with the disorder, although such minor physical anomalies as a highly arched palate or low-set ears may occur at a higher rate in children with ADHD than in the general population. The likelihood of physical injury is also higher in these children, probably due to their increased level of activity. Intellectual development, as assessed by intelligence tests, appears to be slightly lower in children diagnosed with ADHD, but the difference is very small. In many cases, the *DSM-IV* indicates, the difference may simply be due to the fact that the child has

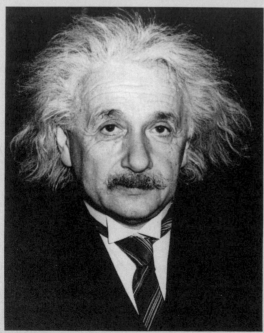

Albert Einstein (1879–1955), recognized as the greatest physicist of all time, is most famous for his theory of relativity and for his role in urging the United States to develop the first atomic bomb during World War II. Einstein suffered from attention-deficit/hyperactivity disorder, and as a result of his struggles with the disorder he had trouble in school and disliked formal education.

difficulty paying attention to exam instructions.

Life with ADHD has been compared, in the *DSM-IV*, to perceptions under a strobe light. Sudden shifts in attention lead to a constantly changing view of the world, which impairs the person's ability to engage in complex thinking, respond emotionally, and learn social rules and guidelines.

In its severest form, the disorder affects an individual's ability to interact with family, friends, and peers and teachers at school. Experiences of failure at school, in sports, and at social activities and chronic struggles at home frequently result in low self-esteem and feelings of misery and resentment from an early age. These children may develop problematic ways to deal with these difficulties, including denial, externalization of blame, withdrawal, regression, and bullying or clowning. Impulsive symptoms may also lead to the breaking of family or school rules, especially in adolescence.

SYMPTOMS OF ATTENTION DEFICIT/HYPERACTIVITY DISORDER

Not all children with ADHD have behavior problems and hyperactivity or are excessively aggressive. The type of ADHD characterized predominantly by inattention is common in psychiatric settings where the threshold for diagnosis requires only minimal aggressive behavior, such as specialty clinics for mood or learning disorders. In contrast to children with the type of ADHD characterized predominantly by hyperactivity, these chiefly inattentive children show mild anxiety and shyness, are more sluggish and less impulsive, display fewer behavior problems, and exhibit symptoms of mood or anxiety disorders.

Following are descriptions based on the *DSM-IV* of the features that make up attention-deficit/hyperactivity disorder:

Inattention can be seen in academic, occupational, or social situations. Youngsters who are inattentive may fail to give close attention to details or may make careless mistakes in schoolwork. Projects are often messy, the child's work habits are disorganized, and the materials necessary for doing the task are often scattered, lost, or damaged. These children typically do not follow through on instructions and often fail to complete chores. School tasks or play activities do not hold their attention. However, inattention should be diagnosed only if failure to complete tasks is not due to other reasons, such as failure to understand the instructions.

Inattentive individuals often seem as if their mind is elsewhere or as if they are not listening to what has just been said. They often have difficulties organizing activities—moving from one to another, then turning to yet something else—without finishing any single task. As a result, these individuals typically dislike activities such as homework or paperwork that demand sustained self-application, organization, or close concentration.

Also common to persons diagnosed with predominantly inattentive ADHD is the tendency to be distracted easily. These children frequently interrupt what they are doing when distracted by trivial noises such as a car honking or a background conversation. Inattention may also be indicated when a child frequently shifts conversation subjects, does not listen to others or attend to conversations, or does not follow the rules of games or activities.

Hyperactivity may vary with age and development level. Hyperactive toddlers and preschoolers, unlike normal young children, are constantly on the go, according to the *DSM-IV*. They dart back and forth, climb on furniture, run through the house, and have a hard time staying still for sedentary activities such as listening to a story.

School-age children display similar behavior, but usually with less frequency or intensity. Hyperactive children have difficulty remaining seated, fidget with objects, tap their hands, and shake their feet or legs excessively. Talking incessantly and making noise during activities that are supposed to be quiet is also common. In adolescents and adults, symptoms of hyperactivity are indicated by feelings of restlessness and reluctance to engage in quiet, sedentary activities.

Children with hyperactivity are active nearly all the time. When children are expected to be active—in the cafeteria, at recess, during gym—both hyperactive and normal children operate at similar levels of activity. However, ADHD children are most different from normal children during structured classroom activities. Even in their quietest moments, children with ADHD are moving: they may fall, bump into things, or knock things over. Clinicians have found that motor activity remains high while the child with ADHD is sleeping; this suggests that inattention is not the primary cause of the problem.

Impulsivity is indicated by impatience: the child blurts out answers before questions have been completed, has a hard time waiting for his or her turn, and frequently interrupts others. These actions are persistent

As a member of the Beatles, arguably the greatest rock-and-roll band ever, John Lennon was considered a musical genius. However, in school Lennon appeared to be bright but a poor student, largely because he suffered from attention deficit/hyperactivity disorder.

enough to cause frustration at home and at school or with playmates. The *DSM-IV* states that individuals with this form of ADHD typically make comments without being asked; fail to listen to directions; initiate conversations at inappropriate times; grab objects from others or touch things they are not supposed to touch; and clown around. Impulsive behavior often leads to accidents like knocking over objects, and many people with this form of ADHD may engage in potentially dangerous activities without consideration of possible consequences.

Disorganization is common in impulsive children with attention-deficit/hyperactivity disorder. Emotional impulsivity, shown by anger and fighting, is often quickly triggered in response to minor provocations.

DIAGNOSTIC CRITERIA FOR ATTENTION DEFICIT/HYPERACTIVITY DISORDER

A. The child meets the conditions in either (1) or (2)

(1) Six (or more) of the following symptoms of inattention have persisted for at least six months.

Inattention

a. often fails to give close attention to details or makes careless mistakes in schoolwork, work, or other activities.
b. often has difficulty sustaining attention in tasks or play activities.
c. often does not seem to listen when spoken to directly.
d. often does not follow through on instructions and fails to finish school-work, chores, or duties in the workplace (not due to oppositional behavior or failure to understand instructions).
e. often has difficulty organizing tasks and activities.
f. often avoids, dislikes, or is reluctant to engage in tasks that require sustained mental effort (such as schoolwork or homework).
g. often loses things necessary for tasks or activities (for example, toys, school assignments, pencils, books, or tools).
h. is often easily distracted by extraneous stimuli.
i. is often forgetful in daily activities.

(2) Six (or more) of the following symptoms of hyperactivity-impulsivity have persisted for at least six months.

Hyperactivity

a. often fidgets with hands or feet or squirms in seat.
b. often leaves seat in classroom or in other situations in which remaining seated is expected.

However, anger is not always the problem. Exploratory behavior can seem aggressive, involving an energetic foraging into new places and things. On entering a room, the child may immediately begin to touch and climb on furnishings. Such inclinations can lead to rough handling of objects, accidental breakage, intrusive behavior, entry into unsafe areas, physical injuries, and accidental ingestions.

    c.   often runs about or climbs excessively in situations in which it is inappropriate (in adolescents or adults, this may be limited to subjective feelings of restlessness).

    d.   often has difficulty playing or engaging in leisure activities quietly.

    e.   is often "on the go" or often acts as if "driven by a motor."

    f.   often talks excessively.

Impulsivity

    g.   often blurts out answers before questions have been completed.

    h.   often has difficulty awaiting turn.

    i.   often interrupts or intrudes on others (for example, butts into conversations or games).

B.   Some hyperactive-impulsive or inattentive symptoms that caused impairment were present before age 7 years.

C.   Some impairment from the symptoms is present in two or more settings (for example, at school and at home).

D.   There must be clear evidence of clinically significant impairment in social, academic, or occupational functioning.

E.   The symptoms are not better accounted for by another mental disorder (for example, mood disorder, anxiety disorder, or schizophrenia or another psychotic disorder).

Source: *Diagnostic and Statistical Manual of Mental Disorders*, fourth edition

DIAGNOSING ADHD

For a person to be diagnosed with ADHD, specific examples of behavior problems must be present in at least two settings, such as at home and at school. However, it is very unusual for an individual to display the same level of dysfunction in all settings or at all times. Symptoms typically become more noticeable in situations that require sustained attention or mental effort. When the child is under strict control, is in an unfamiliar setting, or is engaged in a particularly interesting activity, the signs of the disorder may be minimal or absent. When the child receives frequent rewards for "good" behavior, there is also a decrease in the appearance of symptoms. The behavioral characteristics of attention deficit/hyperactivity disorder are more likely to occur in interactive situations, such as when the person is at play, in the classroom, or at work.

Although most individuals with this disorder have symptoms of both inattention and hyperactivity-impulsivity, there are some individuals in whom one pattern or the other is predominant. The *DSM-IV* divides attention-deficit/hyperactivity disorder into three subtypes: predominantly hyperactive-impulsive, predominantly inattentive, and combined.

1. **Predominantly Inattentive:** There must be six or more symptoms of inattention, as described earlier in the chapter, but fewer than six symptoms of hyperactivity-impulsivity.

2. **Predominantly Hyperactive-Impulsive:** There must be six or more symptoms of hyperactivity-impulsivity, but fewer than six symptoms of inattention.

3. **Combined:** At least six symptoms of inattention and six symptoms of hyperactivity-impulsivity must be present.

Most children and adolescents with attention-deficit/hyperactivity disorder have the combined type.

Usually the disorder is first diagnosed during elementary school years, often when a child's poor adjustment to school shows obvious signs of a problem. It is especially difficult to establish this diagnosis in children younger than age four or five years, because "normal" behavior at this age includes actions that are similar to symptoms of attention-deficit/hyperactivity disorder, according to the *DSM-IV*. In fact, 50 percent of all normal boys at this age are incorrectly considered hyperactive

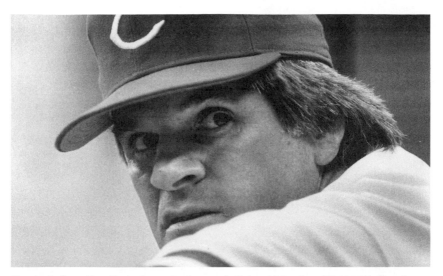

Baseball player Pete Rose, the major leagues' all-time hit leader with 4,256, suffered from attention-deficit/hyperactivity disorder as a child. One of the best baseball players of the 1960s and '70s, Rose was nicknamed "Charlie Hustle" by teammates because he played hard all the time.

by their parents and teachers.

Symptoms of inattention are common among children who are placed in academic settings that are more challenging than they can handle. Inattention in the classroom may also occur when children with high intelligence are placed in class situations that are not stimulating. These children must be distinguished from children with attention-deficit/hyperactivity disorder.

In the majority of cases seen in clinical settings, the disorder is relatively persistent through early adolescence, but as children mature symptoms usually become less conspicuous. Hyperactivity may now be confined to fidgetiness or an inner feeling of restlessness. At this stage, many untreated or treatment-resistant youngsters with ADHD tend to feel embattled and consider themselves failures at school and at home. The relative frequency of late-adolescence conduct difficulties and substance abuse in such youngsters reflects their risk for turning to deviant peer groups or to drug and alcohol use to compensate for feelings of failure, rejection by more adequate peers, and depression.

A substantial proportion of children referred to clinics with attention-deficit/hyperactivity disorder also have oppositional defiant disorder or conduct disorder, which will be discussed in the next chapter.

Oppositional defiant disorder, and to a certain extent conduct disorder, tend to be distinguished by a resistance to rules set forth by parents or authority figures.

4

CONDUCT DISORDER AND OPPOSITIONAL DEFIANT DISORDER

C onduct disorder and oppositional defiant disorder, like attention deficit/hyperactivity disorder, are classified by the American Psychiatric Association as disruptive behavior disorders. However, unlike ADHD, these disorders involve violations of others' rights, confrontation with adults or authority figures, and even violence in some cases.

For children undergoing therapy for these disruptive behavior disorders, a certain amount of anxiety is generated because of the sense of restriction in the clinical environment. Not surprisingly, once a diagnosis is made and therapy begins, individuals with disruptive behavior disorders often rely on defensive mechanisms, such as attempts to control, devalue, intimidate, manipulate, or seduce the therapists, or even attempts to pit parents and therapists against each other. They also may resort to rejecting help, running away, abusing drugs, and intensifying antisocial behavior outside of the sessions.

CONDUCT DISORDER

Repeated violations of the rights of others characterize conduct disorder. Several behavioral patterns may develop from this disorder, ranging from frequent lying, cheating, running away, and truancy, to more serious offenses like vandalism, arson, rape, and armed robbery.

The children or young adults most likely to be diagnosed with conduct disorder often have a history of trauma—particularly physical and sexual abuse or the early loss of a parent or close relation—intersecting with a broad range of other psychological problems, including mood disorders, ADHD, or learning disabilities. Children with conduct disorder are largely inhibited, and

Children with conduct disorder often react aggressively to their peers and may display violent or bullying behavior. These children may also show symptoms of attention deficit disorder or learning disorders.

may be haunted by an inordinate sense of self-responsibility. They may be upset about their symptoms, but they are generally unprepared to acknowledge any inner turmoil.

Children with conduct disorder commonly have low self-esteem, although they often try to hide these feelings with an attitude of bravado or toughness, according to the *DSM-IV*. Another sign of conduct disorder is academic underachievement, which may be related to learning or communication problems, especially reading disorder or expressive language disorder. Individuals with this diagnosis may also resort to alcohol or drug use to combat feelings of anxiety, depression, boredom, or anger—thus complicating the condition by further aggravating already volatile behavior.

SYMPTOMS OF CONDUCT DISORDER

Children and adolescents with conduct disorder may show symptoms of attention deficit disorders or learning disorders, as well as sullen, impulsive, or angry moods. These children may show a lack of sense about events and consequences, and often have weak logical thinking skills.

Children or adolescents with this disorder often initiate aggressive behavior and react aggressively to others, according to the *DSM-IV*. They tend to be physically cruel to people or animals, and may display bullying or intimidating behavior. Physical violence may eventually take the form of assault, rape, or in extreme cases, homicide. Deliberate destruction of others' property is another characteristic feature of conduct disorder, and may include smashing car windows, vandalizing school property, or committing arson intended to cause serious damage.

Characteristically, a person with this disorder often violates parental or school rules. The *DSM-IV* indicates that children with conduct disorder often have a pattern, beginning before age 13 years, of staying out late at night despite parental discipline. There may be occurrences of running away from home overnight (at least twice, or one time for a lengthy period); however, this condition does not apply to children who run away because of physical or sexual abuse. Frequently or unnecessarily missing school, or in older persons, missing work, may be another indicator of conduct disorder.

The severity of the disorder in a particular individual depends greatly on the timing of the first appearance of the symptoms of conduct disorder. For this reason, the American Psychiatric Association divides conduct disorder into two subtypes: childhood onset and adolescent onset.

Childhood-onset type is defined by the onset of at least one of the symptoms of conduct disorder in a child younger than 10 years old. Children with the childhood-onset type of conduct disorder are usually male, frequently display physical aggression toward others, and have a difficult time relating to peers. They may have had oppositional defiant disorder during early childhood, and they usually have symptoms that meet the full criteria for conduct disorder before they reach puberty. These individuals are more likely to have persistent problems with conduct disorder as teens and adults than are children with the adolescent-onset type.

Adolescent-onset type is defined by the absence of any criteria characteristic of conduct disorder before the child is 10 years old. Compared to children with the childhood-onset type of conduct disorder, these individuals are less likely to show aggressive behavior and more likely to have good relationships with peers—although they often display conduct problems. They are also less likely to have problems with conduct disorder as adults. Although boys are more likely to have the adolescent-onset type of conduct disorder than are girls, the ratio of males to females is lower for this type, compared to the childhood-onset type.

CASE STUDY: DIAGNOSING
CONDUCT DISORDER

Joe, a 13-year-old youth diagnosed with conduct disorder, had been subjected to brutal physical and sexual abuse by an alcoholic father, while his mother pursued her theatrical career (Bleiberg, 1994). He had just entered psychiatric therapy and, almost in spite of himself, was beginning to feel more comfortable with his therapist, even looking forward to the sessions.

Yet he had a problem with closeness, and in order to distance himself from others he began to look carefully for mistakes that they had made. He'd erupt into hateful verbal barrages when his therapist interrupted him or "invaded his space" by walking too close. He told the therapist that he planned to run away from the hospital and find the therapist's house, so that he could set the house on fire, after raping the therapist's wife and murdering his children with slow, intravenous injections of cocaine. He assured the therapist that his life would be spared, but only so that the therapist would suffer from the loss of everything he loved.

Joe's tirade spoke volumes about what closeness meant to him. In Joe's mind it could only lead to a painful, destructive invasion of his body and self. The envy Joe felt toward his therapist's possessions and relationships evoked his rage at his own deprivation and abuse, and drove him to crave the elimination of all possible rivals for his therapist's love while leaving the therapist just as deprived, lonely, and needy as himself.

With colorful stories, Joe would project himself as a hardened gang member steeled by life on the mean streets of the big city. Because he considered himself such a fierce, savvy person, he commented that his

There are two types of conduct disorder: adolescent-onset and childhood-onset. Those children who develop conduct disorder early in life typically have more problems as teens and adults than those who develop the disorder during adolescence.

"wimpy, nerdy" therapist couldn't possibly understand him. In reality, Joe had grown up in the far more sedate environment of an upper-middle-class community in New England. His knowledge of gangs had mostly been acquired through extensive reading on the subject.

The therapist countered Joe's stories with an even more fantastic account of his own heroic battles as a gang kingpin—a secret identity that he hid behind his deceptively mild appearance. Joe seemed to enjoy this gambit, and during subsequent sessions he engaged in a good deal of increasingly good-natured bantering. Only after the therapist and Joe had reestablished a relationship at a distance that Joe could more readily tolerate were they able to go back and deal with the rage that Joe had experienced and the abuse he had inflicted on the therapist.

This vignette illustrates how youngsters with conduct disorder often require therapy that creates a transitional area of relatedness—between

Conduct disorder, if untreated in children and adolescents, can develop into a more serious psychological disorder called antisocial personality disorder. A high percentage of people with either disorder have committed a serious crime or been incarcerated by the time they are 26 years old.

fantasy and reality—in which patients can both own and disown their rejected feelings and experiences and test out the therapist's connection, respect, and responsiveness to the vulnerable aspects of the self.

A step in the right direction—toward this necessary therapeutic alliance—helped Joe maintain a sense of control despite his family's and therapist's increasing influence over him. This therapeutic alliance is referred to by clinicians as a *holding environment*. In this way, the patient can more readily accept the therapy itself. As this case illustrates, such tasks involve a delicate balance between fostering adaptive solutions to life's demands, maintaining a semblance of control, and keeping anxiety and shame within manageable limits. Cognitive-based treatments such as this can reduce aggression and antisocial behavior, thus reducing social pressure and helping a youngster gain a measure of control.

POTENTIAL OUTCOMES

The possible complications of conduct disorder are numerous. Consequences can include low tolerance of frustration, loss of interest in school leading to failure to graduate, and subsequent unemployment. Family relationships may suffer. More serious problems may include drug addiction or criminal activities. The individual's physical health may be at risk from suicide attempts or injuries due to fighting. Children with conduct disorder frequently require emergency room visits and hospitalizations. The most common causes of death in those diagnosed with conduct disorder are suicide, motor vehicle accidents, and death from uncertain causes (Rydelius, 1988).

When compared to children with conduct disorder alone, children with conduct disorder that is exacerbated by attention-deficit/hyperactivity disorder tend to have an earlier onset of symptoms, more aggressive behavior, and more severe problems. By the time a person with these disorders reaches age 26, there is a tendency toward more serious crime and a higher rate of incarceration. A 1984 study indicated that 85 percent of imprisoned youths could be diagnosed with conduct disorder, and that about 20 percent had ADHD or a learning disorder. About 50 percent of the prisoners had IQs below 85. The study concluded that criminal activity was more closely related to psychiatric problems or intelligence than to family or economic variables.

However, despite the extremely high incidence of conduct disorder among criminals, about 50 percent of children with conduct disorder are able to achieve a favorable adjustment by adulthood (Loeber, 1982; Rutter and Giller, 1984). In addition, there is a tendency toward a reduction in antisocial symptoms after age 40 (Hare and Jutai, 1988).

Although later onset and good socialization skills may suggest to doctors a better adult outcome for children or young adults diagnosed with conduct disorder, it is unknown to what extent that good outcome is associated with the natural course of illness, life experiences, therapeutic intervention, or preexisting characteristics. Intelligence and a small family appear to offer some level of protection and healing, thus curtailing the persistence of conduct disorder.

DIAGNOSTIC CRITERIA FOR CONDUCT AND OPPOSITIONAL DEFIANT DISORDERS

DIAGNOSTIC CRITERIA FOR CONDUCT DISORDER

A.   A repetitive and persistent pattern of behavior in which the basic rights of others or major age-appropriate societal norms or rules are violated, as manifested by the presence of three (or more) of the following criteria in the past 12 months, with at least one criterion present in the past six months.

Aggression to people and animals

1.   often bullies, threatens, or intimidates others.
2.   often initiates physical fights.
3.   has used a weapon that can cause serious harm to others (for example, a bat, brick, broken bottle, knife, or gun).
4.   has been physically cruel to people.
5.   has been physically cruel to animals.
6.   has stolen while confronting a victim (for example, a mugging, purse snatching, armed robbery, or extortion).
7.   has forced someone into sexual activity.

Destruction of property

8.   has deliberately engaged in fire setting with the intention of causing serious damage.
9.   has deliberately destroyed others' property (other than by fire setting).

Deceitfulness or theft

10.   has broken into someone else's house, building, or car.
11.   often lies to obtain goods or favors or to avoid obligations (i.e., "cons" others).
12.   has stolen items of nontrivial value without confronting a victim (for example, shoplifting, but without breaking and entering; forgery).

Serious violations of rules

13.   often stays out at night despite parental prohibitions, beginning before age 13 years.
14.   has run away from home overnight at least twice while living in parental or parental surrogate home (or once without returning for a lengthy period).
15.   is often truant from school, beginning before age 13 years.

B. The disturbance in behavior causes clinically significant impairment in social, academic, or occupational functioning.

C. If the individual is age 18 years or older, criteria are not met for antisocial personality disorder.

Source: *Diagnostic and Statistical Manual of Mental Disorders*, fourth edition

DIAGNOSTIC CRITERIA FOR OPPOSITIONAL DEFIANT DISORDER

A. A pattern of negativistic, hostile, and defiant behavior lasting at least 6 months, during which four (or more) of the following are present:

1. often loses temper.
2. often argues with adults.
3. often actively defies or refuses to comply with adults' requests or rules.
4. often deliberately annoys people.
5. often blames others for his mistakes or misbehavior.
6. is often touchy or easily annoyed by others.
7. is often angry and resentful.
8. is often spiteful or vindictive.

Note: a criterion is met only if the behavior occurs more frequently than is typically observed in individuals of comparable age and developmental level.

B. The disturbance in behavior causes clinically significant impairment in social, academic, or occupational functioning.

C. The behaviors do not occur exclusively during the course of a psychotic or mood disorder.

D. Criteria are not met for conduct disorder, and if the individual is age 18 or older, criteria are not met for antisocial personality disorder.

Source: *Diagnostic and Statistical Manual of Mental Disorders*, fourth edition

Children with oppositional defiant disorder are often stubborn, resistant to directions, and unwilling to compromise. The disorder occurs in older children and adolescents and usually affects relationships with adults or authority figures, such as teachers, rather than peers.

OPPOSITIONAL DEFIANT DISORDER

Oppositional defiant disorder is marked by persistently negative and defiant behavior that usually becomes evident before age eight years and usually not later than early adolescence. Although the disorder includes some of the features observed in conduct disorder, such as disobedience and opposition to authority figures, it does not include a persistent pattern of more serious forms of behavior in which rules or the basic rights of others are violated.

Children with oppositional defiant disorder express defiant conduct through stubbornness, resistance to directions, and unwillingness to compromise. The self-defeating stand these children often take in arguments indicates their willingness to lose something they want, like a privilege or a toy, rather than to lose a struggle. The struggle takes on a life of its own in the child's mind and becomes more important than the actual situation. Rational objections by the authority figure are counterproductive, and the child may feel that these interventions are actually a continuation of the argument.

Defiance may also include deliberate or persistent testing of limits, usually by ignoring orders, arguing, or failing to accept blame for misdeeds. Hostility can be directed at peers but is usually aimed at adults, and is expressed by deliberately annoying others or by verbal aggression—usually without the more serious physical aggression seen in conduct disorder.

Manifestations of the disorder are almost invariably present in the home setting, but may not be evident at school or in the community. Because signs of oppositional defiant disorder are typically revealed during interactions with adults or peers whom the individual knows well, symptoms also may not be apparent during clinical examination. Usually individuals with this disorder do not regard themselves as defiant, but justify their behavior as a response to unreasonable demands or circumstances.

Symptoms may vary, depending on the individual's age and the severity of oppositional defiant disorder. The disorder is most common among males who showed a volatile temperament or were abnormally hyperactive during their preschool years. During later school years these individuals often have a poor self-image and experience frequent mood swings; they may resort to alcohol, cigarettes, or drug abuse. Inevitably, conflicts with parents increase, exacerbating the problem as parents become more impatient and the child more hostile and defensive.

Oppositional defiant disorder is more prevalent in males than in females before puberty, but the rates seem to be equal after puberty. Symptoms are generally similar in males and females, although males may show more confrontational behavior and their symptoms may be more persistent. In a significant proportion of cases, oppositional defiant disorder later develops into, or is accompanied by, conduct disorder. However, the progression to conduct disorder does not always happen, and even if it does occur it is easier to treat individuals with oppositional defiant disorder successfully, as opposed to those with childhood-onset conduct disorder.

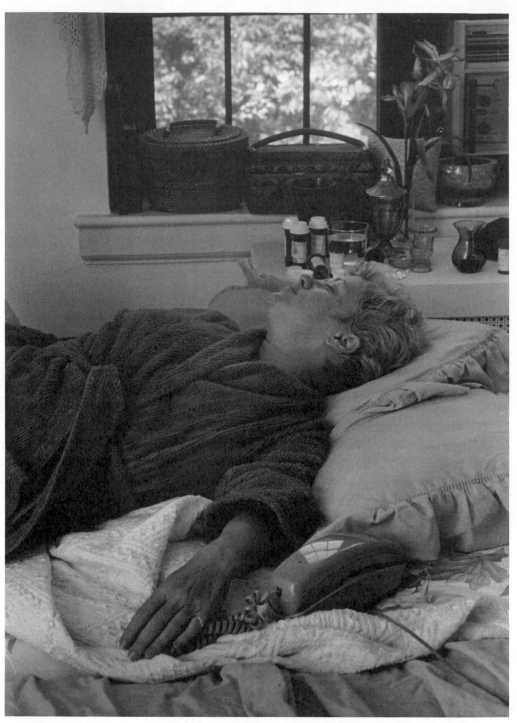

The effects of disruptive behavior disorders can persist into adulthood, including chronic unemployment, substance abuse, depression, and even violent behavior in some cases.

5

THE IMPACT ON SOCIETY

ttention-deficit/hyperactivity disorder (ADHD), conduct disorder, and oppositional defiant disorder constitute the most common psychological conditions diagnosed in children and adolescents. And one of the challenging aspects of child psychiatry is predicting the future significance of symptoms associated with these and other childhood disorders. In other words, which inattentive seven-year-old girl will outgrow her problems by puberty or young adulthood and which will have enduring and impairing attention-deficit/hyperactivity disorder? Which 14-year-old boy with conduct disorder will eventually "fit into society" by adulthood and which will simply decline into severe antisocial behavior? Perhaps more important, what will be the overall impact of children with these conduct disorders on society?

ATTENTION-DEFICIT/ HYPERACTIVITY DISORDER

Attention-deficit/hyperactivity disorder is a major clinical and public health problem in the United States because of its links to other disorders—including conduct disorder and oppositional defiant disorder—and the resulting disability in children, adolescents, and perhaps in adults. The financial costs to society are significant, as ADHD can lead to lost production, underemployment, and the need for reeducation.

Attention-deficit/hyperactivity disorder is also associated with, or may lead to, oppositional defiant disorder and conduct disorder. Studies show that hyperactive preschoolers frequently become conduct-disordered elementary school-age children (Campbell, 1995) and that early-onset conduct disorder is more likely to develop into antisocial personality disorder (Hechtman, 1995), which in adults is characterized by a pattern of disregard for the rights of others and aggressive, violent actions. Juvenile fire-setting is usually associated with attention-deficit/hyperactivity disorder or conduct disorder, and pyromania occurs much more often in males, especially those with poorer social skills and learning difficulties.

The likelihood of developing antisocial personality disorder in adult life is increased if the individual experienced an early onset of conduct disorder (before age 10) accompanied by attention-deficit/hyperactivity disorder. Child abuse or neglect, unstable or erratic parenting, or inconsistent parental discipline may increase the likelihood that this combination will evolve into antisocial personality disorder.

Even though studies show that ADHD persists into adulthood in 10 to 60 percent of childhood-onset cases (Hechtman, 1991; Mannuzza, 1993), little attention has been given to the adult form of this disorder. The high prevalence of attention deficit/hyperactivity disorder among children, combined with these follow-up results, suggests that approximately two percent of adults may suffer from ADHD. This would make ADHD a relatively common adult disorder, and it may be underidentified in adult psychiatry clinics, according to the *Treatment of Psychiatric Disorders*, second edition *(TPD-II)*.

CASE STUDY:
DAVE, AN ADULT WITH ADHD

Dave, 44, a desktop publishing consultant, has on his desk three personal computers, two laser printers, four telephone lines, a fax machine, and 500 little yellow sticky notes calling for his attention. He is often talking on the phone while answering an E-mail, printing out a brochure, and faxing information to a client—all while thinking about something else. "Technology lets me keep up with my mind," he says. "It lets me try my ideas as soon as I can come up with them."

However, Dave has trouble getting anything done. Anytime he receives new information, or is interrupted by a family member, it could cause him to change his focus from the work he is doing. It might be hours, or days, before he returns to the task he had been working on. Dave is an adult with attention deficit disorder.

Individuals with conduct disorder are often confrontational, using "tough" behavior to mask low self-esteem.

As a child, Dave was overactive but not hyperactive enough to cause much trouble. In college, however, he found the less-structured atmosphere harder to cope with. Although he had scored a perfect 800 in math on his SATs, he had such a difficult time with his freshman calculus class that he was advised never to take another math class again. As an adult, Dave finds himself constantly scanning his environment, searching for interesting information. He often starts to read books but never finishes them. He misplaces things and constantly needs to be

The symptoms of conduct disorder–truancy, criminal behavior, and alcohol or drug abuse–tend to worsen as a child with the disorder progresses through adolescence.

reminded about plans or work deadlines. Dave is often late for meetings and usually tries to juggle several projects at once.

This is pretty typical for adults with ADHD, specialists say. However, although adults with ADHD often shift their attention from one task to the next, when something grabs their full attention, they can focus on it for hours. Unfortunately, these adults are not able to control what they pay attention to and what they block out. Not surprisingly, many adults with ADHD are not able to hold down a traditional office job. Many, like Dave, set up their own businesses surrounded by high-technology tools, like computers.

After Dave realized that he had ADHD, he saw a specialist, who prescribed Ritalin as part of his treatment. "The first day I took Ritalin, a thought came into my mind and I said, 'No. It isn't time for that now,' he later told a magazine reporter. "I now have the ability to go back to whatever I was talking about" (Schwartz, 1994).

CONDUCT DISORDER

Those diagnosed with conduct disorder tend to have little empathy or concern for the feelings, wishes, and well-being of others. Individuals with this disorder are likely to misperceive the intentions of others as being more hostile and threatening than is truly the case. They will then respond with an aggression that they feel is justified.

Conduct disorder may be linked with lower-than-average intelligence—a possible contributor to the frequent problem of substandard academic achievement, particularly in reading and other verbal skills, among children with this disorder. The poor tolerance for frustration, in addition to the temper outbursts and recklessness associated with conduct disorder, often leads to verbal bullying of others or to physical assaults.

Studies have shown that people diagnosed with conduct disorder are more likely to engage in sexual contact at a young age, according to the *DSM-IV*. This increases the risk for sexually transmitted diseases and unplanned pregnancy among these young adults. Another problem area is substance abuse, as individuals with this disorder often experiment with drinking, smoking, or using illegal substances at an early age. These behaviors may lead to school suspension or expulsion, problems adjusting to work, and legal difficulties later in life. Illegal drug use in particular may increase the risk that problems of conduct disorder will persist into adulthood.

Individuals with conduct disorder often hurt themselves and those around them by their aggression or recklessness. Accident rates appear to be higher in individuals with conduct disorder than in those without it. Suicidal fantasies, suicide attempts, and even completed suicides also occur at a higher-than-normal rate in individuals with conduct disorder.

Perhaps the most serious consequence of childhood conduct disorder is that in many cases the disorder develops in adulthood into a more serious psychological problem, labeled *antisocial personality disorder* by the American Psychiatric Association. In a 30-year study of 500 child-guidance clinic patients, 37 percent of those who showed antisocial behavior as children developed severe problems in adulthood. These problems included antisocial behavior, alcohol abuse, psychiatric hospitalization, child neglect, financial dependency, and records of poor employment or military service performance. These problems did not appear to be influenced by psychiatric treatment, lengthy incarceration, job or military experiences, or religion; however, there was evidence of improvement when the person was involved in a stable relationship, supported by family members, or held in prison for a brief period.

In a separate study of 9,945 Philadelphia boys with conduct disorder, 35 percent had been arrested by their 18th birthdays, and 6 percent became chronic offenders. These young adults accounted for a large percentage of the prison population (Wolfgang, 1972). Repeat offenders in this sample had early-onset conduct disorder, poor school grades, and low socioeconomic status.

These studies indicate that people who have conduct disorder negatively impact their communities. Coupled with the problems that result with attention deficit/hyperactivity disorders, conduct disorder has a serious effect on society today.

OPPOSITIONAL DEFIANT DISORDER

There is little evidence that oppositional defiant disorder by itself is a problem for society. This is partly due to the fact that oppositional behavior is a typical feature of the normal development of the personality at certain stages, usually during early childhood and again during adolescence. The disruptive behavior that individuals with oppositional defiant disorder exhibit is less severe than that exhibited by those with conduct disorder. These individuals typically do not act aggressively toward people or animals, destroy property, or develop a pattern of theft or deceit.

Further, while most oppositional symptoms, such as arguing, disobedience, and defiance, typically peak between the ages of 8 and 11 years and then decline in frequency, symptoms of conduct disorder—truancy, stealing, alcohol use—tend to worsen as the child goes through adolescence. Consequently, because the course of conduct disorder often worsens with age, concern arises when oppositional defiant disorder is found to coexist with conduct disorder, resulting in a much more troublesome psychological condition.

Although disruptive behavior disorders like ADHD, conduct disorder, and oppositional defiant disorder are fairly common, the exact causes of these conditions remain unknown.

6

CAUSES OF DISRUPTIVE BEHAVIOR DISORDERS

Despite the widespread occurrence of attention-deficit/hyperactivity disorder, conduct disorder, and oppositional defiant disorder, there is much uncertainty regarding their origins and causes. The field of psychiatry is still grappling with how best to treat these disorders, but until specific causes can be determined, treatment will continue to be based on case reports and general studies.

The questions researchers and clinicians ask are these: To what degree does family history, including genetic transmission and behavior learned within the family setting, affect the onset of these disorders? And how important are environmental factors in causing or exacerbating—and, ideally, in alleviating—the associated symptoms?

The possibility exists that each of these disorders may stem from a common root, even though their courses and outcomes differ. Some researchers have attempted to determine where they diverge; much research has been devoted to analysis of where the disorders and the associated behavioral problems overlap. Many proposals are supported by reliable, thorough studies, while other theories remain mere speculation in need of additional supporting evidence. Until more conclusive results are attained, new studies will continue to explore and defend hypotheses of the causes of these disorders.

ATTENTION-DEFICIT/HYPERACTIVITY DISORDER

It is believed that ADHD has multiple causes, stemming more from neurological and genetic factors than from purely social influences. There is convincing evidence that ADHD is linked to diminished activity in certain regions of the brain caused by genetic transmission—that is, inherited from

The characteristics of attention deficit/hyperactivity disorder run in families—particularly in boys. Although ADHD may have a genetic component, the family environment also has a major effect on development of the disorder.

parents—or early trauma. Attention-deficit/hyperactivity disorder is not caused by parental failure to discipline or control a child.

Attention deficit/hyperactivity disorder runs in families, particularly in males. In adopted children with ADHD, the biological parents often have a greater history of psychiatric problems than do the adoptive parents. Studies also suggest that family members of individuals with ADHD are more likely to have conduct disorder, mood and anxiety disorders, learning disorders, drug-related disorders, or antisocial personality disorder. This holds true even after the populations of these studies are controlled to eliminate the effects of socioeconomic class and family instability.

There may be subgroups of children with ADHD who have other associated psychiatric disorders as well. Attention deficit/hyperactivity disorder is not infrequent among individuals with Tourette's syndrome, which often begins in childhood and causes facial, body, and vocal tics (such as involuntary swearing). When the two disorders coexist, the onset of attention-deficit/hyperactivity disorder often precedes the onset of Tourette's. There may be a history of child abuse or neglect, multiple foster home placements, infections such as encephalitis, drug exposure in utero, and mental retardation.

Some children with ADHD have a parent with a history of, or current symptoms of, a similar condition. However, there is no evidence that a single genetically transmitted brain mechanism is responsible for ADHD. The hereditary component is likely to be explained as the result of a specific combination of genes. Although more large-scale follow-up genetic studies are needed, it appears that in many children, the cause of ADHD is rooted in their genes.

Doctors believe there are a variety of other possible causes for ADHD, including brain damage, neurological disorders, low birth weight, and fetal exposure to toxins. Occasionally, children with the syndrome have clear evidence of damage to their central nervous system at birth. Obstetrical problems during pregnancy or delivery, such as bleeding or lack of oxygen, can also cause neurological damage. However, difficulties during pregnancy and birth probably only account for a tiny percentage of ADHD cases.

Prenatal factors are probably more important than birth problems in the etiology, or cause, of these psychiatric disorders. For example, children with low birth weights are more likely to develop ADHD, whether or not there are additional complications during delivery. If a fetus is exposed to toxic substances, including alcohol and lead, this can produce abnormal effects on behavior. For example, symptoms of fetal alcohol syndrome include hyperactivity, impulsivity, and inattention, as well as physical anomalies. Prenatal and postnatal toxic exposure to lead can precede ADHD and other learning disabilities, and children with attention-deficit/hyperactivity disorder often have chronically higher levels of lead in their blood than siblings without the disorder. A large-scale study in Ottawa showed that a large number of children with ADHD children lived in public housing, leading observers to theorize that the lead-based paints used on the walls of these apartments may contribute to development of ADHD.

Severe early malnutrition is probably the most common cause of ADHD-like symptoms. In children who experience severe malnutrition during the first year of life, 60 percent show inattention, impulsivity, and hyperactivity through childhood and young adulthood (Galler et

There is no one gene that causes the attention deficit/hyperactivity disorder; instead, doctors believe a combination of genes is responsible. Factors other than genetics, such as low birth weight, fetal exposure to drugs or alcohol, or damage to the brain or central nervous system, also contribute to ADHD.

al., 1983).

If chronic medical conditions are treated with certain drugs, a drug-induced form of ADHD can result. Symptoms of inattention, hyperactivity, or impulsivity that are related to the use of medication in children younger than age seven do not merit a diagnosis of attention-deficit/hyperactivity disorder.

Clinicians believe that girls constitute 10 to 25 percent of children with attention deficit/hyperactivity disorder, although this may be an underestimate. Data on ADHD in girls and women are sparse, because nearly all ADHD research has been conducted on boys; however, there are indications that women may constitute a higher proportion of the adult ADHD population and may seek treatment more frequently than do men, according to a 1985 study that originally appeared in the journal *Pediatrics*. The family psychiatric histories of girls and boys with ADHD appear to be similar. However, girls with attention deficit/hyperactivity disorder appear to show more fear, depression, or mood swings, and cognitive and language problems (Berry et al., 1985).

One surprising fact that researchers found when examining attention deficit/hyperactivity disorder is that ADHD is more likely to be related to genetics in girls than it is in boys (Vandenberg et al., 1986). Several theories have been postulated to account for this "gender gap." For example, the profiles of ADHD causes or symptoms may be affected by biological gender-related differences, or cultural differences may influence the incidence or recognition of aggressive/hyperactive behavior in boys and girls.

This large array of causal factors contributes to the complexity of the clinical syndrome of ADHD and the difficulties in defining its boundaries. New studies that employ behavioral characteristics, neurological information, drug response, family psychiatric history, and social variables could shed light on these areas. Until then, attention-deficit/hyperactivity disorder will remain defined by purely behavioral criteria, obscuring a multidimensional array of causes.

CONDUCT DISORDER

Conduct disorder is seen in 40 to 70 percent of children with attention-deficit/hyperactivity disorder, so a large portion of the literature on ADHD discusses the combination of ADHD and conduct disorder. Children with the type of attention-deficit/hyperactivity disorder characterized predominantly by inattention only occasionally have conduct disorder, suggesting that the aggressive behavior often seen with conduct disorder is linked to the hyperactive/impulsive element and not to the inattentive element of ADHD. Children with the combination of ADHD and conduct disorder often come from families where several members have psychological disorders, whereas children with the type of ADHD characterized predominantly by inattention may suffer from neurological disorders, lower IQ, and other cognitive deficits.

At its root, conduct disorder has both genetic and environmental components. The risk for conduct disorder is increased in children who have a biological parent with a history of attention-deficit/hyperactivity disorder or conduct disorder, or a sibling with conduct disorder. The disorder also appears to be more common in children whose biological parents are alcoholics or suffer from mood disorders or schizophrenia.

Genetic studies suggest that some factors predisposing children to conduct disorder are inherited; however, studies of twins who have grown up separated in different households suggest that environmental factors are also significant contributors. The characteristics of a child's home environment may lead to the development of conduct disorder. Some of these characteristics include parental neglect, inconsistent child-rearing practices combined with harsh discipline, a lack of supervision, frequent change of caregiver, and large family size. Adding to the risk are an absent or alcoholic father, parental abandonment, physical or sexual abuse, and association with a delinquent peer group—the "wrong crowd."

Coming from a broken home does not appear to be a major risk factor, and despite the increase in single-parent homes, family discord—rather than separation—appears to increase the risk for conduct disorder (Lahey et al., 1988).

The presence of certain positive factors in the home environment can counteract many of these negative influences. For example, adequate supervision in the home, especially when parents are away, can reduce the risk for conduct disorder.

In certain children with conduct disorder, especially more aggressive and violent children, neurological factors may have a greater causal role. The degree of aggressive behavior may correlate with a history of physical abuse, head and face injuries, neurological abnormalities, ADHD, and possibly problems at birth. In extremely violent youth, severe learning and communication problems are common. A series of studies conducted in the 1980s indicates that seizures occur in 20 percent of these children, compared to less than 1 percent in the normal population, and psychotic symptoms appear in 60 percent, compared to about 2 percent in the general population (Lewis et al., 1982; Lewis et al., 1988).

Some doctors and social workers have raised concerns that a diagnosis of conduct disorder may be misapplied to individuals in settings where patterns of undesirable behavior might more accurately be viewed as protective. In threatening, impoverished, or high-crime settings, certain behaviors associated with the disorder may be necessary for survival. The *DSM-IV* gives the example of an immigrant youth from a war-ravaged country who has a history of aggressive behaviors—fighting, stealing—that may have been necessary for survival in that country. This youth's behavior would not necessarily warrant a diagnosis of conduct disorder, because it should be diagnosed only when a child's behavior indicates an underlying dysfunction within the individual, and not a reaction to his or her surroundings.

Although three-quarters of the children with attention deficit/hyperactivity disorder are boys, clinicians believe that women may compose a higher percentage of the adult population with ADHD. Most of the research into the disease has been done on boys, but one study indicated that girls with attention deficit/hyperactivity disorder seemed to exhibit more fear, depression, and mood swings and had more problems with language than did their male counterparts.

OPPOSITIONAL DEFIANT DISORDER

At present, there is no systematic evidence that would permit identification of a unique cause or even a variety of causes for oppositional defiant disorder as there is with attention-deficit/hyperactivity disorder and conduct disorder. Perhaps as a result, speculations abound. One of the first documented theories came out in 1955, when Dr. Eugene Levy, in his book *Oppositional Syndromes and Oppositional Behavior in Psychopathology of Childhood*, suggested that markedly oppositional behavior occurs as a reaction of the child to overly strict parenting. More than two decades later, oppositional behavior was interpreted as

Children with a biological parent who has a history of ADHD or conduct disorder, is a substance abuser, or suffers from a mood disorder have an increased risk of developing conduct disorder.

the youngster's response to "a restrictive and demanding parental environment" (Meeks, 1979). More recent theories suggest that the main causes of oppositional defiant disorder are negative reinforcement of inappropriate child behavior through inadequately resolved parent-child conflict, particularly about issues of control and autonomy (Gard and Berry, 1986; Patterson et al., 1989).

The *DSM-IV* indicates that oppositional defiant disorder is more common in families in which at least one parent has a history of psychological problems. These problems may include mood disorder, oppositional defiant disorder, conduct disorder, attention-deficit/hyperactivity disorder, antisocial personality disorder, or a substance-related disorder. In addition, some studies indicate that mothers with a depressive disorder are more likely to have children with oppositional behavior; however, it is unclear to what extent maternal depression causes oppositional behavior in children. The *DSM-IV* notes that "oppositional defiant disorder is more common in families in which there is serious marital discord."

Oppositional defiant disorder may be the result of many factors, alone or in combination, including genetic, physical, social, and psychological causes, indicates the *Comprehensive Textbook of Psychiatry*. In the absence of direct studies identifying the cause of this disorder, the following psychological and social factors constitute the more widely accepted hypotheses today:

1. parental problems in disciplining, structuring, and limit setting
2. identification with an impulse-disordered parent who sets an example for oppositional and defiant interactions with other people
3. parental unavailability, perhaps due to separation or erratic work hours

However, neurobiological influences and temperamental factors may also contribute.

Preliminary studies suggest a familial influence on oppositional defiant disorder, but more research is needed to determine whether it is mainly genetically transferred, caused by a child's environment (for example, through family interaction) or both.

A combination of medication and therapy is commonly used to treat children who are diagnosed with attention deficit/hyperactivity disorder. With treatment, many of these children go on to lead normal lives.

7

TREATING ATTENTION DEFICIT/HYPERACTIVITY DISORDER

I ndividuals with disruptive behavior disorders can be treated: some with medication, some with therapy. The effectiveness of any treatment program, however, depends on many variables. Of course, in order for an individual to overcome a disruptive behavior disorder, he or she must first be accurately diagnosed. And as these disorders reveal themselves in childhood and adolescence, the symptoms must be recognized by both parents and teachers, and proper actions taken.

Treatment for disruptive behavior disorders is *multimodal,* meaning that the disorders are treated by a combination of modes, such as medication and therapy. Treatment begins with education of the parents, children, and teachers about the disorder. This is particularly important in differentiating symptoms of hyperactivity and inattention from oppositional behaviors. A combination of behavior therapy and medication is most commonly used in the treatment of disruptive behavior disorders. A trial of a medication, usually a stimulant such as methylphenidate or dextroamphetamine, is often initiated. For older children, cognitive-behavioral therapy may assist the child in developing strategies to minimize impulsive behavior (Kendall and Braswell, 1985).

This chapter will examine some of the common methods for treating attention deficit/hyperactivity disorder, while Chapter 8 will focus on the treatment of conduct disorder and oppositional defiant disorder.

ATTENTION-DEFICIT/HYPERACTIVITY DISORDER

Attention-deficit/hyperactivity disorder is a widely encountered diagnosis—too widely, according to some people. It is possible that some children are

Diagnosing ADHD may be difficult, because what seems to be hyperactive or inattentive behavior may actually be normal childhood behavior. Other environmental factors may also lead to an incorrect diagnosis. A thorough examination is required to rule out other possible causes for the inattention or hyperactivity before ADHD is diagnosed and an appropriate treatment plan determined.

inaccurately identified as having ADHD, and this can lead to inappropriate treatment. Some evaluators may not notice alternative or coexisting causes for observed behavior that is symptomatic of ADHD. Possible contributors to a false ADHD diagnosis are the presence of language disorders, learning problems, agitation due to depression, previous traumatic brain injury, or a dysfunctional home. For example, a child's anxious response to a dysfunctional home situation may be similar to ADHD behavior. Also, certain medications, such as those used to treat asthma, can contribute to hyperactivity and inattention. A clinician must evaluate these factors carefully, because for different patients the appropriate treatment may differ. A thorough evaluation is required to rule out other possible diagnoses before determining an appropriate treatment plan.

Given the high rates of conditions coexisting with attention-deficit/hyperactivity disorder, there is relatively little research on "pure" ADHD. After excluding ADHD children who also have learning disorders, conduct disorder, mood and anxiety disorders, or Tourette's syndrome from a study population, one might wonder whether ADHD could possibly even exist in pure form. One hypothesis suggests that the existence of accompanying disorders, rather than the ADHD itself, may be responsible for the severity of symptoms, and that children with the pure form of ADHD may just be viewed as "energetic," and not need treatment.

A congenital disorder or early-onset disorder, such as attention-deficit/hyperactivity disorder, can also be modified by life experiences. Biological and genetic influences that are prominent during early childhood may be "washed over" in time by social and environmental factors. As a child grows, socioeconomic class, family environment, education, and access to medical treatment become increasingly important influences on behavior and personality. Attention deficit/hyperactivity disorder characteristics can be amplified into more severe psychiatric problems, or they can be channeled into useful energetic activity, depending on these factors.

THE ROLE OF THE FAMILY

Families with one or more children who have attention-deficit/hyperactivity disorder experience considerable stress due to the child's difficulties with attention and impulses, hyperactivity, and emotional reactivity. The parents and the general quality of family life are substantially affected by these children. Doctors today believe that a multidimensional approach, which involves treating both the child and the family, offers the best chance for long-term success. The parents must be taught "child management techniques" that include incentives for good social behavior and consistent use of consequences, clearly outlined for the child, when unacceptable behavior occurs. The children themselves can benefit from efforts to learn specific social skills.

The following story, originally part of a study published in the *Journal of Psychotherapy Practice and Research*, illustrates one example of such treatment strategies:

The family is considerably affected when a child has a disruptive behavior disorder, and the family plays an important role in the treatment of attention deficit/hyperactivity disorder. Parents must learn and utilize consistent disciplinary techniques that reward children for good social behavior and punish them for unacceptable behavior.

The Atkins family and their eight-year-old daughter Anita were referred by a medical clinic for family therapy. Anita was diagnosed with attention deficit/hyperactivity disorder, and had a tendency to withdraw in social situations involving people other than her family members. The parents needed to work on management techniques. The therapist alternated sessions with the entire family—Anita, her parents, and her younger brother—with one-on-one sessions with Anita.

The therapist began each session by meeting with the parents to discuss progress and goals. Management and communication techniques were practiced in the family sessions, and the parents and children worked together to negotiate "behavior contracts" that provided rewards when acceptable behavior goals were met.

During the family portion of the session, the parents presented their behavioral expectations for both Anita and her brother. They discussed consequences of behavioral choices, and the parents listened carefully to encourage input from both siblings. And to ensure communication and consistency between parents and teachers, the therapist guided the parents in making decisions about the school Anita should attend and attended meetings with her teachers at the school.

Individual sessions were geared toward increasing Anita's independence, sense of responsibility, and self-esteem. The therapist was also working with the family's physician so that medication dosages (Anita was being treated with methylphenidate) could be modified as needed.

During the treatment, Anita's mother became aware of her own ADHD characteristics and requested an evaluation by a separate therapist. Both therapists met with her after the evaluation to discuss individual needs and family dynamics. A few individual sessions helped Mrs. Atkins to increase her self-understanding and to reach out for social support, producing positive benefits in her parenting and family relationships. Sessions occurred less and less frequently during the next several months, and the treatment moved toward termination as the family progressed and Anita made a positive adjustment in school (Cordell and Allen, 1997).

EVALUATION AND MONITORING

To assess the possibility that a child has attention-deficit/hyperactivity disorder, clinicians obtain the child's family history; information from school such as grades, behavior, peer relationships, and results of achievement testing; and a diagnostic interview of the child. Completion of standard parent rating scales such as the Abbreviated Parent Questionnaire and ADD-H: Comprehensive Teacher's Rating Scale (ACTeRS) is also helpful (Conners, 1970; Ullmann et al., 1984). The doctor may decide that psychological evaluation, educational assessment, or speech and language testing may also be necessary because of the frequent association of ADHD with specific develop-

The school environment is one of the most important sources of information about a child who may have attention deficit/hyperactivity disorder. In addition to grades and the results of achievement tests, doctors need to know how well the child interacts with peers.

mental disorders such as speech and language problems and developmental arithmetic disorders.

It is unlikely that any rating scale has the clinical usefulness of a combination of reports from a variety of settings: home, school, and day care.

To monitor the effectiveness of treatment, behavioral reports are requested from teachers. The Child Attention Problems profile (CAP) is sensitive to both inattention and hyperactivity/impulsivity factors and can yield a score that is sensitive to the effects of stimulant medications. The older Conners Teachers Questionnaire is widely employed but is a nonspecific measure of misbehavior and conduct problems; it is also not as useful for monitoring the type of attention-deficit/hyperactivity disorder predominantly characterized by inattention. The Home Situations Questionnaire (HSQ), which can be used by parents or residential caregivers, assesses behaviors in a variety of different settings and can also measure drug effects (Barkley, 1990).

Treatment outcomes are best evaluated by speaking with parents, teachers, and observers in different settings. Rather than relying on clinical interviews in a quiet office where ADHD behaviors may be least evident, a more effective instrument for evaluating a child's treatment for attention-deficit/hyperactivity disorder is often the telephone.

MEDICATION

For children with ADHD, doctors often prescribe medications to improve attention span and impulse control. Medication can help reduce a child's activity level, increase compliance with rules (good behavior), help a child to get along better with peers, and improve a child's focus on school tasks. The same treatments are apparently successful in adults with ADHD, although there is not a lot of information about this population.

When a child begins taking medication to counter a disruptive behavior disorder like ADHD, his or her pulse, blood pressure, height, and weight are monitored regularly so that any possible adverse effects can be quickly detected. In addition, teachers and parents complete behavior rating scales before and after each dosage change to assist in assessment of drug response.

Drug treatment often continues for several years, with regular adjustments in the dosage of medication necessary to counteract changes in the child's body weight, varying environmental or developmental stress, or changes in the rate of absorption of the drug. In some cases, treatment is no longer required by the time of adolescence, but many individuals show a continuing need for treatment into adulthood.

Stimulants such as dextroamphetamine (Dexedrine), methylphenidate (Ritalin), and pemoline (Cylert) are the most popular drugs in the treatment of children of normal intelligence with attention-deficit/hyperactivity disorder.

Dextroamphetamine is a short-acting stimulant that can be effective in treating apathy and inattention. It also has the advantage of being

Drugs such as the stimulants dextroamphetamine and methylphenidate have been found to be effective in helping treat attention deficit/hyperactivity disorder. However, stimulant treatment is merely one part of a larger program of therapy.

generally cheaper than other psychostimulants. Methylphenidate is an alternative drug that has a longer duration—anywhere from 8 to 12 hours. Methylphenidate is, in some cases, preferred over dextroamphetamine because it does not have the same side effects on the treated person's cardiovascular system, including increased pulse and blood pressure. Dextroamphetamine also has a higher potential for abuse, and a greater risk of growth retardation.

Of the available stimulants, dextroamphetamine and methylphenidate are a bit more effective and safer than magnesium pemoline. However, pemoline generally needs to be administered only once a day, although absorption and metabolism vary widely and some children may need twice-daily doses. But the possibility for pemoline-induced chemical hepatitis, although rare, requires monitoring of liver enzymes and thus

HISTORY OF DRUG TREATMENT OF ADHD

The first documented mention of the use of stimulant medication for children with school and behavior problems was in a 1937 article by Charles Bradley, M.D. The article described the dramatic results in some of the children he treated with benzedrine. This discovery led directly to the success of the use of stimulants in the treatment of what now is termed attention deficit/hyperactivity disorder but was, for decades, ignored by the medical profession (*American Journal of Psychiatry,* 1995).

Dr. Bradley was the medical director of a small hospital for children with major difficulties in learning, behavior, or both. Some of the children had clear-cut neurological disorders; others appeared to have "emotional problems." Today the latter would probably be diagnosed with oppositional defiant disorder, conduct disorder, or attention deficit disorder. Dr. Bradley chose the most potent stimulant available at the time, benzedrine, to treat the headaches of the children in his hospital. To his astonishment, the teachers reported major improvements in learning and behavior in a number of the children, which lasted until the benzedrine regimen was withdrawn. The children themselves noted the greater ease of learning and called the medication "math pills," presumably because mathematics was the hardest subject for them, and their improved ability to learn was most noticeable in that subject. With this serendipitous result, the next step was a systematic trial in 30 of the children residing in his hospital. Half of them showed dramatic improvement in learning and behavior; they were more interested in their work and performed more quickly and accurately.

Dr. Bradley's discovery was revolutionary. He continued to use benzedrine in his hospital, but no one else attempted to replicate his findings until the early 1960s. He also continued to experiment with other drugs, and soon methylphenidate was found to be effective. After this, the use of stimulants to treat children with minimal brain dysfunction, hyperkinetic syndrome, and attention deficit disorder began to increase.

limits the usefulness of magnesium pemoline for certain patients (Sallee et al., 1985).

Another commonly prescribed stimulant is clonidine. Although it's not effective in treating inattention, clonidine has been proven useful in modulating mood and activity level and improving cooperation and frustration tolerance in children with ADHD, especially those who are hyperactive, impulsive, defiant, or emotionally unstable.

Children taking stimulants may show side effects such as anorexia, insomnia, or anxiety, but enough children with attention-deficit/hyperactivity disorder benefit from the drug treatment to warrant closely monitored use of stimulants.

Studies of adults who show symptoms resembling those seen in children with ADHD have revealed that these adults may respond well to stimulant therapy (Wender et al., 1985; Huessey, 1979). These drug responders are very likely to have been considered "hyperkinetic" children. Although many children with ADHD seem to grow out of the major manifestations of the disorder at some time in adolescence, some individuals who have had clear clinical benefit from stimulants in childhood continue to require, and to benefit from, stimulant medication well into adulthood.

Tricyclic antidepressants (TCAs) are an alternative for those patients who do not respond to stimulants or who develop significant depression while on stimulants. It has been shown that patients who have ADHD and an accompanying anxiety disorder may respond better to a TCA than to a stimulant (Kutcher et al., 1992). Low doses of antidepressants like nortriptyline are said to provide therapeutic effects that last more than 24 hours, but the actual duration of effects may be shorter. The longer duration of action of TCAs means that doses of medication do not have to be given during the day, when the child is at school. However, the effectiveness in improving cognitive symptoms like inattention does not appear to be as great with TCAs as with stimulants. Other drawbacks to TCAs include the possibility of relapse or resistance to the treatment; potentially serious cardiac side effects, especially in prepubescent children; and an increased danger of accidental overdose when doses are taken at intervals closely spaced together.

Initial studies of tricyclic antidepressants used imipramine. A drawback to this drug is that it causes an anticholinergic effect, meaning that it affects performance of the nerves. However, another TCA, desipramine, has been found to have less of an anticholinergic effect in addition to well-documented, long-term effectiveness (Biederman et al., 1989).

The psychostimulant treatment of ADHD does present a public policy problem, as amphetamines and methylphenidate are highly abusable. More than 95 percent of prescriptions for amphetamines are for

Adjusting the environment of a child with ADHD is another method of minimizing the symptoms of the disorder. Parents can attempt to reduce distractions by creating quiet spaces in the home, encouraging fine motor exercises like putting together puzzles, and limiting social interactions to one friend at a time.

diet control, and many people feel these drugs should be withdrawn from the market. Better education about the use of these medications, along with the development of less abusable treatments such as antidepressants, might provide a solution to the problem. The risks of this childhood disorder probably exceed the potential risks of even long term pharmacological treatment, but drug treatment alone is insufficient for the majority of patients, many of whom need psychiatric assistance.

ENVIRONMENTAL ADJUSTMENTS

Adjusting the individual's surroundings is another useful method for minimizing ADHD symptoms. Parents and teachers can help reduce distractions and sensory overstimulation by modifying the patient's home and school settings. For children at home, parents are advised to establish quiet spaces, decorate with simple furniture and subdued colors, and keep toys put away in a closet. Encouraging fine motor exercis-

Unfortunately, relationships are often strained in families in which a child suffers from attention deficit/hyperactivity disorder. Feelings of resentment may come out during therapy, making resolution of the problems caused by ADHD more difficult.

es like putting together jigsaw puzzles is also useful. Parents can regulate social interaction by permitting visits by only one friend at a time and avoiding exposing the child to crowded settings like supermarkets and parties.

Because children with ADHD typically fall below the educational level expected for their school grade, special education or tutoring is generally required. At school, a small classroom, group activities, thoughtful selection of seating location (near the front of the room, away from doors and windows where activity may be distracting), routine and predictable structure, one-on-one tutoring, and use of a "resource room" where children can perform various interesting and educational activities can be beneficial. Supervised or modified recess, gym, bus, and cafeteria arrangements are also effective. Transitions to new schools and between programs requires a little foresight. Informing school officials about the child's strengths, problems, and social skills and receiving regular reports regarding behavior and academic performance are essential. An individualized educational plan (IEP) can be developed with the child's teacher or with the school in order to facilitate classroom arrangements. The IEP may include strategies that deal with learning disorders related to the disruptive behavior disorder.

Adults suffering from ADHD can also organize their workspaces and set up their daily schedules to maximize productivity. They can set up appointments and meetings for predetermined lengths of time and at periods during the day when their attention span is typically at its peak. If possible, their workplaces should be located in low-traffic areas, where few distractions exist.

NONPHARMACOLOGICAL THERAPY

If medications and environmental adjustment do not lead to improved behavior, academic or job performance, or social adjustment, then additional psychiatric treatments should be considered. *Behavior therapy* is employed for treatment of defiance and aggressivity. Behavioral methods can be as effective as psychostimulants for modifying classroom behavior, but do not carry over well to other situations and are more costly.

Behavior therapy is the most effective treatment for simple phobias and for the noncompliant behaviors seen in oppositional defiant disorder and conduct disorder. For youngsters with ADHD, behavior modification can improve both academic achievement and behavior, if these are specifically targeted. To be fully effective, behavior modification must include both punishment and reward components. Behavior modification is more effective than medication in improving peer interactions, but certain skills may have to be taught first. Many youngsters require programs that are consistent, intensive, and prolonged. These treatment programs can last a year or more.

Cognitive-behavior therapy is used to teach problem-solving strategies, self-monitoring, verbal mediation (using encouraging internal speech for self-praise or instruction), and seeing, rather than glossing over, errors. Education and support for parents and family members are crucial and can be provided through programmed group-training sessions.

Methylphenidate in combination with behavior modification at home and school has been shown to have a positive effect on motor, attention, and social measures for many, but not all, children with attention-deficit/hyperactivity disorder. Although a sufficiently intensive and structured behavioral program will nearly normalize the classroom behavior of children with ADHD, 30 to 60 percent of children will improve further with the addition of low-dose methylphenidate (Pelham and Murphy, 1986). The combination of such classroom behavior therapy as token economy (giving rewards, or tokens that can be exchanged for rewards, for good behavior), time-outs, and daily report cards with a low dose of methylphenidate can produce results similar to those produced by a high dose of medication alone (Carlson et al., 1992). This is particularly important when medication side effects are problematic. Behavior modification addresses symptoms that are not addressed by stimulants, although a greater commitment from parents and teachers is required.

DIFFICULTIES IN TREATING ADHD

Doctors have encountered many difficulties when treating children with attention deficit/hyperactivity disorder. Family relationships are often characterized by resentment and antagonism, especially because variability in the individual's symptoms may lead parents to believe that all the troublesome behavior is willful. Exacerbating this situation is the fact that parents often come to depend on the medication rather than making needed changes in the environment. Although stimulants are frequently a necessary and effective supplement to therapy, they should be considered just that—a *supplement*. Attention is required to avoid possible side effects of therapy, such as lower self-esteem and stigmatization by peers. Both patients and adults who are significant in patients' lives can be instructed that medication enables the patient to accomplish what he or she wishes to do, just as eyeglasses help someone to see; it does not make him or her do anything. It is especially important that patients are given full credit for improvement and helped to take an appropriate amount of responsibility for problems that arise.

Certain treatments have been examined but not widely accepted. Studies on the Feingold diet, which involves omitting salicylates (a salt compound) and food dyes, have yielded contradictory findings, but food dye restriction might be helpful for 5 to 10 percent of children with attention-deficit/hyperactivity disorder. Various other dietary treatments have been considered, but they have not been proven effective in large-scale studies.

Some forms of behavior therapy have proven ineffective. For example, individual therapy is much more likely to be effective for children and adolescents who are in emotional distress or who are struggling to deal with a stressor than for those children with behavior problems. Children and adolescents with attention-deficit, oppositional, or conduct disorders rarely acknowledge their problem behavior and are usually better treated in family or group therapy, by parent training in behavior management, or in a structured milieu. Youngsters with ADHD have little insight into their behavior and its effect on others, and may be genuinely unable to report some of their problems or to reflect on them. Insight-oriented therapy may be useful for some of these youngsters, however, to address associated anxiety or depression, or symptoms resulting from psychological trauma.

The scarcity of available data on attention-deficit/hyperactivity disorder in adults leaves many gaps in knowledge of this disorder and its treatment into and beyond adolescence. In a reversal of the pattern common in psychiatry in which knowledge from the study of adult psychological disorders informs and often distorts the initial approach to the psychiatric treatment of children, the treatment of ADHD in adults is unfortunately based largely on speculations and on some confirmed inferences based on studies in children. With findings of significant adult psychopathology in attention-deficit/hyperactivity disorder accumulating, the traditional view of this disorder as a benign childhood condition is being vigorously reexamined.

■　　　　　■　　　　　■

It seems clear that ADHD may result from a large variety of causes and that various syndromes ultimately lead to behavioral hyperactivity and inattention. The features of ADHD are so diverse that it is unlikely that any single set of interventions will treat or prevent more than a small fraction of cases. Subtyping on the basis of behavioral criteria alone is only half the battle, probably in part due to of the associated effects of coexisting psychiatric and neurological problems, familial-genetic psychiatric history, and familial and social variables. Unless and until attention-deficit/hyperactivity disorder is separated into subgroups incorporating psychiatric, neurological, familial, genetic, and psychosocial markers, stimulants will likely remain a necessary part of overall treatment for all those who suffer from the disorder.

Proper treatment, utilizing individual and family therapy as well as drug therapy, can resolve the problems of many children who are diagnosed with a disruptive behavior disorder.

8

TREATING OTHER
DISRUPTIVE BEHAVIOR
DISORDERS

C onduct disorder is an umbrella term that unifies a tremendous diversity of disorders derived from biological, psychological, familial, and social factors under a single name. As with ADHD, until clinicians can determine specific methods to treat subgroups of conduct disorders, treatment of youngsters with the disorder will remain largely generic, rather than directed to address individual cases. The actual treatment of children with conduct disorder is based on a variety of child-rearing and psychiatric treatment philosophies.

The difficulty in treating conduct disorder stems from its associated behavioral traits. Children with this disorder show excessive aggression, manipulation, arrogance, and defiance and an apparent lack of guilt. These are characteristics that are far more likely to elicit feelings of anger and helplessness from a parent than feelings of empathy and concern. Furthermore, the seeming lack of suffering and interest in change, and the absence of a serious psychiatric impairment like a mood disorder, in these children strains a therapist's ability to justify the necessity for a tortuous, lengthy, and often unsuccessful treatment.

The following information from a case report originally published in *Review of Psychiatry* highlights the initial treatment of a 15-year-old boy hospitalized because of conduct disorder:

Robert began therapy with a superficial eagerness to solve his problems. However, such therapeutic zeal soon gave way to rather flamboyant expressions of contempt for the hospital, the hospital's treatment team, and the therapist. He had expected that a famous clinic would provide him with a therapist perfectly suited to treat him—a "perfect match." Robert had some hope on first meeting his therapist that it was such a match because he noticed they both had blue eyes and blond hair. He was quickly disappointed, however, when he heard the therapist's obviously foreign accent. He could not understand why he had been subjected to the ignominy of having a "spic" for a therapist. The therapist commented that his Hispanic accent seemed to represent inferiority to Robert—a flaw with which he would be embarrassed to be associated.

"Not bad for a spic," he replied, quickly turning to his doubts about whether "spics" could understand the concerns of someone of obviously superior Nordic descent, such as he was. At that point his therapist mentioned that Robert seemed to be saying that if they were not identical—not only in looks but in backgrounds as well—he would not be able to understand and appreciate Robert. "Not bad for a spic," was again his response. Yet a budding relationship could be detected in his mocking compliment.

This relationship, of course, was only tentative. Nonetheless, Robert confided his concerns that if he trusted his therapist, the therapist would find a way to sabotage Robert's plans to "behave appropriately" and maintain a "positive attitude." Such behavior would, he was sure, convince the clinical staff and his parents that he was ready to return to his beloved home state, instead of enduring the disgrace of rotting in dreadful Kansas. This comment, of course, betrayed Robert's own efforts to effectively use manipulation and pretense to solve his problems. (Kestenbaum and Lewis, 1994)

The presence of some form of collaborative relationship allows therapists to gently encourage their patients to consider an expansion in the range of shareable experiences. Narcissistic youngsters are invited to share their experiences of vulnerability, depression, pain, helplessness, and dependency. Borderline and impulsive children are introduced to the notion of continuity of the self and to relationships. Depressed patients are encouraged to look at the restrictions in their play and emotional range.

Therapists' acknowledgment of the utter terror children feel as they enter into a rejected, dissociated, denied aspect of their lives and relationships can prevent therapeutic stalemates and limit regression. Therapists should always point out the disadvantages of not changing—in effect, the price children would pay if they were to retain their abnormal but often protective defenses. Ultimately, therapists present to their patients, implicitly or explicitly, a therapeutic bargain: If you relinquish

The attitudes of teens with conduct disorder toward forbidden substances like drugs, cigarettes, or alcohol, their aggressive or defiant behavior, and a lack of apparent guilt make them difficult for parents to understand, complicating treatment.

the pathological defenses and the illusion of control and safety that these defenses provide—and commit to a far more exposed and laborious process of self-examination—you will be rewarded with real mastery of your life and meaningful relationships with others.

Parenting has a great impact on the treatment of children with oppositional defiant disorder. Child management techniques are necessary in order to help children overcome this disorder, which if untreated often develops into a more serious psychological problem.

In addition, a family therapist can provide a different perspective and help an individual's psychotherapist assess the consequences to the family of the patients' relinquishment of symptoms and the anxieties that those changes may trigger. Involving parents in the treatment serves to address a major source of resistance to treatment: the child's overwhelming anxiety that his or her growth and change will shatter the family and cause the parents to hurt one another, divorce, commit suicide, or abandon the child.

An essential aspect of any psychological treatment program is the drawing of boundaries. Creating or reinforcing limits may necessitate counseling and psychiatric treatment of parents, while the child may require increased supervision at home and at school. The use of such legal mechanisms as guardianship, hearings before judges, counseling by parole officers, and brief incarceration is sometimes necessary for communicating the significance of behavioral violations.

Cognitive-behavior therapy can help a child develop skills for managing anger, controlling impulse problems, and communicating. Training in problem-solving skills may be more effective than individual psychotherapy, and specific methods that target conduct disorder are increasingly used. Parents can help by making decisions concerning management of difficult behaviors and by setting limits on impulsive behavior. Family therapy is useful in certain cases for reducing the child's manipulative tendencies. Psychiatric treatment of parents or siblings is often needed for these family members' own psychiatric disorders. Group therapy, particularly in residential treatment or group-oriented facilities, often permits the "gang orientation" to promote positive overall change and to improve socialization skills.

In school settings, interventions can include special attention to behavioral control, individualized educational programming—especially for language and learning disorders—and vocational training. There is evidence that the early treatment of learning disorders may help prevent the development of conduct disorder.

Maintaining effective limits and focused orientation toward treatment may challenge not only families but also mental health professionals and legal systems. For those patients who resist usual treatment, careful attention may be needed to establish understanding of their view of life and to help them develop a motivation for change. Failure to diagnose an additional psychiatric disorder in the child or the family is a common source of poor outcome. When necessary, parent counseling involves helping parents use the legal system, avoid defending their child's actions, or, in extreme cases, accept the "loss" of the child to a life of imprisonment, crime, or fugitive status.

TREATING OPPOSITIONAL DEFIANT DISORDER

Oppositional defiant disorder can be diagnosed after age three but usually appears in late childhood. Follow-up studies suggest that 40 percent of children with oppositional defiant disorder will retain the symptoms for at least four years (Cantwell and Baker, 1989). Certain individuals undergo a developmental progression from oppositional defiant disorder to attention-deficit/hyperactivity disorder, conduct disorder, or other psychiatric disorders.

Psychiatric evaluation of the child and family is conducted to investigate family and psychosocial factors that may contribute to the child's disorder. An assessment is also done to rule out possible conduct disorder, ADHD, and mood disorders. It is also worthwhile to evaluate for a learning or language disorder or low IQ, which can contribute to the child's oppositional behavior.

There are very few systematic studies of the treatment of children with oppositional defiant disorder. The most recent is a 1988 report by Wells and Egan showing that parent training based on the psychiatric theory of social learning—a belief that the environment, as well as conditioning, affects learning, and a person can modify their environment—was helpful in reducing oppositional behavior. In clinical practice this disorder is treated with a variety of psychological and behavioral approaches, targeting the child and often the entire family as well. Typical approaches include child psychotherapy, behavior therapy, various types of family therapy, and parent management training. No study has identified the utility of medication for children with oppositional defiant disorder; however, pharmacological treatment is believed to be effective in those with coexisting attention-deficit/hyperactivity disorder.

■   ■   ■

Disruptive behavior disorders, such as ADHD, conduct disorder, and oppositional defiant disorder, are not uncommon disorders. In fact, it's quite possible that a family member, neighbor, or classmate suffers from a disruptive behavior disorder, as more than 5 percent of the school-age population have been diagnosed with one of these disorders.

Attention deficit/hyperactivity disorder or one of the other syndromes discussed in this book can greatly affect a person's life, as well as the lives of those around him. However, when the problem is diagnosed accurately, and a plan of treatment is established and followed closely, most patients have been able to overcome the disorder and lead normal lives. In addition, medical professionals continue to study these diseases of the mind and test new strategies of treatment, meaning that some day there may be a cure for all who suffer from a disruptive behavior disorder.

APPENDIX

FOR MORE INFORMATION

Parents of children and adolescents with psychiatric disorders, together with mental health professionals and teachers, have established national organizations that provide education and support for parents, as well as advocacy services and research facilities. Many of these national groups also have local chapters that focus on a particular disorder and serve as a powerful adjunct to direct clinical services.

Adult Attention Deficit Foundation
132 North Woodward Avenue
Birmingham, MI 48009
(810) 540-6335

American Academy of Child and Adolescent Psychiatry (AACAP)
3615 Wisconsin Avenue NW
Washington, DC 20016-3007
(202) 966-7300

The Attention Deficit Information Network
475 Hillside Avenue
Needham, MA 02194
(617) 455-9895

Canadian Mental Health Association (CMHA)
970 Lawrence Avenue West, Suite 205
Toronto, Ontario, M6A 3B6
(416) 789-7957

Children and Adults with Attention Deficit Disorders (CHADD)
499 NW 70th Avenue, Suite 308
Plantation, FL 33317
(800) 233-4050

CHADD (In Canada)
#214—1376 Bank Street
Ottawa, Ontario, K1H 1B3
(613) 731-1209

Kennedy Krieger Institute
707 North Broadway
Baltimore, MD 21205
(888) 554-2080

Learning Disabilities Association of America (LDAA)
4156 Library Road
Pittsburgh, PA 15234
(412) 341-1515

Learning Disabilities Association of Canada (LDAC)
323 Chapel Street, Suite 200
Ottawa, Ontario K1N 7Z2
(613) 238-5721

National Alliance for the Mentally Ill Child and Adolescent Network (NAMI-CAN)
200 North Glebe Road, Suite 1015
Arlington, VA 22203-3754
(800) 950-NAMI

National Attention Deficit Disorder Association (ADDA)
P.O. Box 972
Mentor, OH 44061
(800) 487-2282

National Information Center for Children and Youth with Disabilities
P.O. Box 1492
Washington, DC 20013
(800) 695-0285

NAWA (an alternative to traditional education)
17351 Trinity Mountain Road
French Gulch, CA 96033
(800) 358-NAWA

APPENDIX

FAMOUS PEOPLE WITH ATTENTION DEFICIT DISORDER

Although not all these famous people have been officially diagnosed, they have exhibited many of the symptoms of attention deficit disorder, attention-deficit/hyperactivity disorder, and learning disorders. The point of this list, compiled by the Kitty Petty ADD/LD Institute, is to inspire those with similar challenges.

Hans Christian Anderson
Ludwig van Beethoven
Harry Belafonte
Alexander Graham Bell
Cher
Agatha Christie
Winston Churchill
John Corcoran
Tom Cruise
Walt Disney
Thomas Edison
Albert Einstein
Dwight D. Eisenhower
F. Scott Fitzgerald
Henry Ford
Galileo Galilei

Danny Glover
Whoopi Goldberg
Stephen Hawking
Mariel Hemingway
Dustin Hoffman
Bruce Jenner
Earvin "Magic" Johnson
John Lennon
Carl Lewis
Greg Louganis
John F. Kennedy
Steve McQueen
Wolfgang Amadeus Mozart
Luci Baines Johnson Nugent
Louis Pasteur
General George Patton

Nelson Rockefeller
Pete Rose
Charles Schwab
George C. Scott
George Bernard Shaw
Tom Smothers
Suzanne Somers
Sylvester Stallone
Jackie Stewart
Jules Verne
Leonardo da Vinci
Lindsay Wagner
Robin Williams
Woodrow Wilson
Henry Winkler

APPENDIX

SOURCES CITED

Aichhorn, August. *Wayward Youth*. New York: Meridian Books, 1955. (Original publication: *Internationaler Psychoanalytischer*. Vienna: Verlag, 1925).

Anderson, J. C., S. Williams, R. McGee, et al. "DSM-III Disorders in Preadolescent Children: Prevalence in a Large Sample from the General Population." *Archive of General Psychiatry* 44 (1987).

Barkley, R. A. *Attention Deficit Hyperactivity Disorder: A Handbook for Diagnosis and Treatment*. New York: Guilford Press, 1990.

Berry, C. A., S. E. Sharwtiz, and B. Shaywitz. "Girls with Attention Deficit Disorder: A Silent Minority? A Report on Behavioral and Cognitive Characteristics." *Pediatrics* 76 (1985).

Biederman, J., R. J. Baldessarini, V. Wright, et al. "A Double-blind Placebo Controlled Study of Desipramine in the treatment of ADD, I: Efficacy." *Journal of the Academy of Child and Adolescent Psychiatry* 28 (1989).

Bleiberg, Efrain. "Neurosis and Conduct Disorders." *Review of Psychiatry* 13 (1994).

Buchholz, E. S. "The Legacy from Childhood: Considerations for Treatment of the Adult with Learning Disabilities." *Psychoanalytic Inquiry* 7 (1987).

Campbell, S. "Hyperactivity in Preschoolers: Correlates and Prognostic Implications." *Clinical Psychology Review* 5 (1995).

Cantwell, D. P. "Oppositional Defiant Disorder." In *Comprehensive Textbook of Psychiatry*, 5th ed., vol. 2, edited by Hi Kaplan and B. J. Sadock. Baltimore: Williams & Wilkins, 1989.

Cantwell, D. P., and L. Baker. "Stability and Natural History of DSM-III Childhood Diagnoses." *Journal of the Academy of Child and Adolescent Psychiatry* 28 (1989).

Carlson, C., William E. Pelham, R. Milich, et al. "Single and Combined Effects of Methylphenidate and Behavior Therapy on the Classroom Performance of Children with Attention-Deficit Hyperactivity Disorder."

Journal of Abnormal Child Psychology 20 (1992).

Christiansen, K. "A Review of Studies of Criminality Among Twins." In *Biosocial Bases of Criminal Behavior*, edited by S. Mednick and K. Christiansen. New York: Gardner, 1977.

Cloward, R. A., and L. Ohlin. *Delinquency and Opportunity*. Chicago: Free Press, 1960.

Conners, C. K. "Symptom Patterns in Hyperkinetic, Neurotic, and Normal Children." *Child Development* 41 (1970).

Cordell, A. S., and S. Allen. "Integration of Therapeutic Approaches in Working with Children." *Journal of Psychotherapy Practice* 6 (winter 1997).

Edelbrock, C. "Behavioral Checklists and Rating Scales." In *Basic Handbook of Child Psychiatry*, vol. 5, edited by J. D. Noshpitz. New York: Basic Books, 1987.

Gabbard, Glen O. *Psychodynamic Psychiatry in Clinical Practice: The DSM-IV Edition*. Washington, D.C.: American Psychiatric Press, 1994.

Galler, J. R., F. Ramsey, G. Solimano, et al. "The Influence of Early Malnutrition on Subsequent Behavioral Development, II: Classroom Behavior." *Journal of the American Academy of Child Psychiatry* 22 (1983).

Gard G. C., K. Berry. "Oppositional Children: Taming Tyrants." *Journal of Clinical Child Psychology* 15 (1986).

Hare, R., and J. W. Jutai. "Psychopathy and Cerebral Asymmetry in Semantic Processing." *Personality and Individual Differences* 9 (1988).

Hauser P., A. J. Zametkin, P. Martinez, et al. "Attention Deficit-Hyperactivity Disorder in People with Generalized Resistance to Thyroid Hormone." *New England Journal of Medicine* 328 (1993).

Hechtman, L. "Resilience and Vulnerability in Long Term Outcome of Attention Deficit Hyperactive Disorder." *Canadian Journal of Psychiatry* 36 (1991).

Hechtman, L., and D. R. Offord. "Long-term Outcome of Disruptive Disorders." *Child and Adolescent Psychiatry* 3 (1995).

Huessey, H. "Clinical Explorations in Adult MBD." In *Psychiatric Aspects of Minimal Brain Dysfunction in Adults*, edited by L. Bellak. New York: Grune & Stratton, 1979.

Johnson, A. M., E. Falstein, S. A. Szurek, et al. "School Phobia." *American Journal of Orthopsychiatry* 11 (1941).

Johnson, A., and S. A. Szurek. "The Genesis of Antisocial Acting Out in Children and Adults." *Psychoanalysis Quarterly* 21 (1952).

Kendall, P. C., and L. Braswell. *Cognitive-Behavioral Therapy for Impulsive Children*. New York: Guilford, 1985.

Kestenbaum, C. J., and O. Lewis. "Psychotherapy with Children and Adolescents. *Review of Psychiatry* 13, no. 4 (1994).

Kutcher, S. P., S. Reiter, D. M. Gardner, et al. "The Pharmacotherapy of Anxiety Disorders in Children and Adolescents." *Psychiatry Clinical North America* 15 (1992).

Lahey, Benjamin B., William E. Pelham, Elizabeth Schaughency, et al. "Dimensions and Types of Attention Deficit Disorder." *Journal of the Academy of Child and Adolescent Psychiatry* 27 (1988).

Levy, D. M. "Oppositional Syndromes and Oppositional Behavior." In *Psychopathology of Childhood*, edited by P. Hoch and J. Zubin. New York: Grune & Stratton, 1955.

Lewis, D. O. "Neuropsychiatric Vulnerabilities and Violent Juvenile Delinquency." *Psychiatry Clinical North America* 6 (1983).

Lewis D. O., Harold Pincus, B. Bard, et al. "Neuropsychiatric, Psychoeducational and Family Characteristics of 14 Juveniles Condemned to Death in the United States." *American Journal of Psychiatry* 145 (1988).

Lewis, D. O., Harold Pincus, S. S. Shanok, et al. "Psychomotor Epilepsy and Violence in a Group of Incarcerated Adolescent Boys." *American Journal of Psychiatry* 139 (1982).

Loeber, Rolf. "The Stability of Antisocial and Delinquent Childhood Behavior." *Child Development* 53 (1982).

Mannuzza, S., R. G. Klein, A. Bessler, et al. "Adult Outcome of Hyperactive Boys: Educational Achievement, Occupational Rank, and Psychiatric Status." *Archive of General Psychiatry* 50 (1993).

Meeks, J. E. "Behavioral and Antisocial Disorders." In *Basic Handbook of Child Psychiatry*, vol 2, edited by J. D. Noshpitz. New York: Basic Books, 1979.

Nader K., and R. S. Pynoos. "Parental Report of Children's Responses to Life Threat." Paper presented at the American Psychiatric Association annual meeting, Washington, D.C., May 1992.

Patterson, G. *Coercive Family Process*. Eugene, Ore.: Castilia Press, 1982.

Patterson, G., B. D. DeBaryshe, and E. Ramsey. "A Developmental Perspective on Antisocial Behavior." *American Psychology* 44 (1989).

Patterson, G., J. B. Reid, and T. J. Dishion. *Antisocial Boys*. Eugene, Ore.: Castilia Press, 1992.

Pelham, William E. Jr., and H. A. Murphy. "Attention Deficit and Conduct Disorders." In *Pharmacological and Behavioral Treatment: An Integrative Approach*, edited by M. Hersen. New York: Wiley, 1986.

Redl, F., and D. Wineman. *The Aggressive Child*. Glencoe, Ill.: Free Press, 1957.

Rutter M., and H. Giller. *Juvenile Delinquency: Trends and Perspectives*. New York: Guilford, 1984.

Rydelius, P. A. "The Development of Antisocial Behaviour and Sudden Violent Death." *Acta Psychiatrica Scandinavia* 77 (1988).

Sallee, F., R. Stiller, J. Perel, et al. "Oral Pemoline Kinetics in Hyperactive Children." *Clinical Pharmacology Therapy* 37 (1985).

Schwartz, Evan I. "Interrupt-Driven." *Wired* 2 (1994).

Spencer, T., J. Biederman, and T. Wilens. "Pharmacotherapy of Attention-Deficit/Hyperactivity Disorder: A Life Span Perspective." In *Review of Psychiatry*, vol 16. Washington, D.C.: American Psychiatric Press, 1996.

Ullmann, R. K., E. Sleator, and R. L. Sprague. "A New Rating Scale for Diagnosis and Monitoring of ADD Children." *Psychopharmacology Bulletin* 20 (1984).

Vandenberg, S., S. M. Singer, and D. Pauls. *The Heredity of Behavior Disorders in Adults and Children*. New York: Plenum, 1986.

Wells, K. C., and J. Egan. "Social Learning and Systems Family Therapy for Childhood Oppositional Disorder: Comparative Treatment Outcome." *Comprehensive Psychiatry* 29 (1988).

Wender, P. H., F. W. Reimherr, D. Wood, et al. "A Controlled Study of Methylphenidate in the Treatment of Attention Deficit Disorder, Residual Type in Adults." *American Journal of Psychiatry* 142 (1985).

Winnicott, D. W. "The Antisocial Tendency." In *Collected Papers*. New York: Basic Books, 1958.

Wolfgang, M., R. M. Figlio, and T. Cellin. *Delinquency in a Birth Cohort*. Chicago: University of Chicago Press, 1972.

APPENDIX

FURTHER READING

Aichhorn, August. *Wayward Youth.* New York: Meridian Books, 1955. (Original publication: *Internationaler Psychoanalytischer.* Vienna: Verlag, 1925).

American Psychiatric Association. *Diagnostic and Statistical Manual of Mental Disorders,* 4th edition. Washington, D.C.: American Psychiatric Press, 1994.

———. *DSM-IV Sourcebook,* 3 vols. Washington, D.C.: American Psychiatric Press, 1996.

———. *Manual of Clinical Psychopharmacology,* 2nd edition. Washington, D.C.: American Psychiatric Press, 1991.

———. *Textbook of Neuropsychiatry,* 2nd edition. Washington, D.C.: American Psychiatric Press, 1992.

———. *Textbook of Psychiatry,* 2nd edition. Washington, D.C.: American Psychiatric Press, 1994.

———. *Textbook of Psychopharmacology.* Washington, D.C.: American Psychiatric Press, 1995.

———. *Treatment of Psychiatric Disorders,* 2nd edition. 2 vols. Washington, D.C.: American Psychiatric Press, 1995.

Barkley, R. A. *Attention Deficit Hyperactivity Disorder: A Handbook for Diagnosis and Treatment.* New York: Guilford Press, 1990.

Cloward, R. A., and L. Ohlin. *Delinquency and Opportunity.* Chicago, Ill.: Free Press, 1960.

Gabbard, Glen O. *Psychodynamic Psychiatry in Clinical Practice: The DSM-IV Edition.* Washington, D.C.: American Psychiatric Press, 1994.

Hersen, M., ed. *Pharmacological and Behavioral Treatment: An Integrative Approach.* New York: Wiley, 1986.

Kaplan, Hi, and B. J. Sadock, eds. *Comprehensive Textbook of Psychiatry,* 5th ed., vol 2. Baltimore: Williams & Wilkins, 1989.

Kendall, P. C., and L. Braswell. *Cognitive-Behavioral Therapy for Impulsive Children*. New York: Guilford, 1985.

Noshpitz, J. D., ed. *Basic Handbook of Child Psychiatry*, vol 5. New York: Basic Books, 1987.

Patterson, G. *Coercive Family Process*. Eugene, Ore.: Castilia Press, 1982.

Patterson, G., J. B. Reid, and T. J. Dishion. *Antisocial Boys*. Eugene, Ore.: Castilia Press, 1992.

Redl, F., and D. Wineman. *The Aggressive Child*. Glencoe, Ill.: Free Press, 1957.

Rutter M., and H. Giller. *Juvenile Delinquency: Trends and Perspectives*. New York: Guilford, 1984.

Vandenberg, S., S. M. Singer, and D. Pauls. *The Heredity of Behavior Disorders in Adults and Children*. New York: Plenum, 1986.

Attention deficit/hyperactivity disorder (ADHD): A syndrome of learning and behavioral problems characterized by a combination of symptoms, including inattention, hyperactivity, impatience, and impulsiveness.

Antisocial personality disorder: A psychological disorder in adults that is characterized by a pervasive pattern of disregard for, and violation of, the rights of others. Teens with conduct disorder may develop antisocial personality disorder as they enter adulthood.

Behavior therapy: A form of therapy, based on the principles of learning, in which rewards are given when undesirable behavior patterns and responses are exchanged for desirable responses. This is also called behavior modification.

Conduct disorder: A psychological disorder that is characterized by breaking of rules and in some cases, violence. There are two types of conduct disorder: the childhood-onset type, which is the less serious of the two, and the adolescent-onset type.

Disruptive behavior disorders: A group of disorders that are usually diagnosed in childhood or early adolescence. These include attention deficit/hyperactivity disorder, conduct disorder, and oppositional defiant disorder.

Encephalitis: An inflammation of the brain.

Hyperactivity: The state, or condition, of being excessively active.

Hyperkinetic: Characterized by fast-paced, frenetic activity; hyperactive.

Impulsiveness: Characterized by impatience; a symptom of attention deficit/hyperactivity disorder. For example, a child who blurts out answers before questions have been completed, has a hard time waiting for his turn, and frequently interrupts others may have a problem with impulsiveness.

Inattention: A symptom of attention deficit/hyperactivity disorder. Inattention may be present when a child frequently shifts conversation subjects, does not listen to others or keep his or her mind on the conversation, or does not follow the rules for games or activities.

Learning disabilities: Psychological disorders that affect, or interfere with, the learning process. Examples include dyslexia, reading disorder, or mathematics disorder.

Mood disorders: Psychological disorders, such as depression or bipolar disorder, that are characterized by a disturbance in mood or feeling.

Oppositional defiant disorder: A disruptive behavior disorder, less serious than conduct disorder, that is characterized by a consistent pattern of disobedient, argumentative, or stubborn behavior.

Stimulant: Any drug or agent (such as caffeine) that produces a temporary increase in the activity of an organism. Stimulants such as dextroamphetamine, methylphenidate, or magnesium pemoline are used to treat psychological disorders such as attention deficit/hyperactivity disorder.

Tourette's syndrome: A rare disease characterized by involuntary tics and uncontrollable use of obscene language. Named for a French physician, Georges Gille de la Tourette, who studied the disease early in the 20th century.

Tricyclic antidepressants (TCAs): A group of antidepressant drugs, including imipramine, amitriptyline, and desipramine, that are used to treat psychological disorders such as attention deficit/hyperactivity disorder.

APPENDIX

INDEX

Abbreviated Parent Questionnaire, 71

ADD-H: Comprehensive Teacher's Rating Scale, 71

Adolescent-onset conduct disorder, 17

Aichhorn, August, 22

American Psychiatric Association, 9, 12
    antisocial personality disorder and, 54
    attention-deficit/hyperactivity disorder and, 21
    conduct disorder and, 17, 37, 39-40
    oppositional defiant disorder and, 25, 37

Amphetamines, 76-77
    for attention-deficit/hyperactivity disorder, 21, 76

Antidepressants, for attention-deficit/hyperactivity disorder, 73, 76

Antisocial personality disorder, 50, 54

Attention deficit disorder, 21

Attention-deficit/hyperactivity disorder (ADHD), 9, 12, 13-15, 27-29, 88
    in adults, 13-14, 50-53, 79, 81
    antisocial personality disorder and, 50
    birth problems and, 59
    causes, 14, 57-61
    combined subtype, 22, 27, 34
    with conduct disorder, 15, 35, 37, 43, 49-50, 54, 61

diagnosis, 11-12, 15, 22, 32-33, 34-35, 67-69
drug-induced, 60
famous people with, 9
gender and, 14-15, 58, 60-61
genetic causes, 57-58, 59, 69
history, 21-22
impact on society, 49-53
life experiences and, 69
malnutrition and, 59-60
with oppositional defiant disorder, 19, 35, 49, 88
predominantly hyperactive-impulsive subtype, 22, 27, 29, 30-33, 34
predominantly inattentive subtype, 22, 27, 29-30, 32, 34, 61
prenatal factors, 59
prevalence, 14-15, 50
school setting and, 78-79
symptoms, 15, 29-33
Tourette's syndrome and, 58-59

Attention-deficit/hyperactivity disorder (ADHD), treatment of, 22, 67-81
    in adults, 81
    diet, 80-81
    environment and, 77-79
    family and, 69-71, 81
    home setting and, 77-78
    medication, 12, 21, 53, 67, 71, 73-77, 79-80, 81
    therapy, 67, 79-80, 81

Behavior therapy
    for attention-deficit/hyperactivity disorder, 69, 79-80, 81

for oppositional defiant disorder, 88
Benzedrine, for attention-deficit/hyperactivity disorder, 75
Bradley, Charles, 75

Child Attention Problems profile, 72
Childhood-onset conduct disorder, 17
Clonidine, for attention-deficit/hyperactivity disorder, 75-76
Cognitive-behavior therapy
    for attention-deficit/hyperactivity disorder, 67, 79
    for conduct disorder, 87
Conduct disorder, 9, 12, 16-17, 37-38
    adolescent-onset, 17
    adult-onset, 40
    antisocial personality disorder and, 50, 54
    attention-deficit/hyperactivity disorder with, 15, 35, 37, 43, 49-50, 54, 61
    causes, 17, 61-62
    childhood-onset, 17, 39-40, 47, 50, 53-54
    diagnosis, 12, 17, 40-43, 44-45
    environment and, 61-62
    family interaction models, 23
    gender and, 17, 23, 39, 40
    genetic causes, 61-62
    history, 22-23
    impact on society, 53-54
    neurological models, 23, 61
    oppositional defiant disorder and, 19, 47, 55
    prevalence, 17, 23
    sociocultural models, 22-23
    symptoms, 39-40
Conduct disorder, treatment of, 83-87
    legal mechanisms for, 86
    school setting and, 87
    therapy, 22, 37, 40-43, 83-87

Conners Teachers Questionnaire, 72-73
Cylert, for attention-deficit/hyperactivity disorder, 74-75

Desipramine, for attention-deficit/hyperactivity disorder, 76
Dexedrine, for attention-deficit/hyperactivity disorder, 67, 73-74
Dextroamphetamine, See Dexedrine
Diagnostic and Statistical Manual of Mental Disorders (DSM-IV)
    attention-deficit/hyperactivity disorder and, 27, 29-33, 34
    conduct disorder and, 38, 39, 44-45, 53, 62
    oppositional defiant disorder and, 45, 64-65
Diet, attention-deficit/hyperactivity disorder and, 80-81
Disruptive behavior disorders, 9, 12

Environment
    attention-deficit/hyperactivity disorder and, 77-79
    conduct disorder and, 61-62

Family
    attention-deficit/hyperactivity disorder and, 69-71
    oppositional defiant disorder and, 63-65
Family therapy
    for attention-deficit/hyperactivity disorder, 81
    for conduct disorder, 86, 87
    for oppositional defiant disorder, 88
Feingold diet, 80
Fetal alcohol syndrome, 59

Genetics
    attention-deficit/hyperactivity disorder and, 57-58, 59, 61, 69

conduct disorder and, 61-62
Group therapy
    for attention-deficit/hyperac-
      tivity disorder, 81
    for conduct disorder, 87

Hallowell, Edward M., 27
Home Situations Questionnaire, 73
Hyperactivity syndrome, 21
Hyperkinetic syndrome, 21

Imipramine, for attention-
    deficit/hyperactivity disorder, 76
Insight-oriented therapy, for
    attention-deficit/hyperactivity
    disorder, 81

Lead, attention-deficit/hyperactivi-
    ty disorder and, 59
Levy, Eugene, 24, 63

Medication, for attention-
    deficit/hyperactivity disorder,
    12, 21, 67, 71, 73-77, 79-80, 81
Methylphenidate. *See* Ritalin
Minimal brain damage/dysfunc-
    tion, 21

Nortriptyline, for attention-
    deficit/hyperactivity disorder, 76

Oppositional defiant disorder, 9, 12,
    17-19, 37, 46-47
    attention-deficit/hyperactivity
      disorder with, 19, 35, 49, 88
    causes, 18, 63-65
    conduct disorder and, 19, 47, 55

diagnosis, 12, 18, 25, 45
family and, 63-65
gender and, 18-19, 47
history, 23-24
impact on society, 54-55
prevalence, 18-19
symptoms, 47
therapy, 37
treatment, 37, 87-88

Parenting, oppositional defiant dis-
    order and, 63-65, 88
Parent rating scales, 71
Pemoline. *See* Cylert

Ritalin, for attention-deficit/hyper-
    activity disorder, 12, 53, 67, 74,
    75, 76, 79-80

School setting
    attention-deficit/hyperactivity
      disorder and, 78-79
    conduct disorder and, 87
Stimulants, for attention-
    deficit/hyperactivity disorder, 67,
    73-77, 80, 81

Therapy
    for attention-deficit/hyperac-
      tivity disorder, 67, 79-80, 81
    for conduct disorder, 22, 37,
      40-43, 83-87
    for oppositional defiant disor-
      der, 88
Tourette's syndrome, 58-59

Von Economo's encephalitis, 21

APPENDIX

PICTURE CREDITS

page

8:   Photo Researchers, Inc.
10: Photo Researchers, Inc.
13: Shirley Zeiberg Photography
14: Photo Researchers, Inc.
16: Shirley Zeiberg Photography
20: Shirley Zeiberg Photography
23: Shirley Zeiberg Photography
24: Shirley Zeiberg Photography
26: Terry Wild Studio
28: (top) The National Archives,
     (bottom) Corbis-Bettmann
31: UPI/Corbis-Bettmann
35: UPI/Corbis-Bettmann
36: Photo Researchers, Inc.
38: Photo Researchers, Inc.
41: Photo Researchers, Inc.
42: courtesy Drug Enforcement
     Agency
46: Photo Researchers, Inc.
48: Shirley Zeiberg Photography
51: Shirley Zeiberg Photography

52: Photo Researchers, Inc.
56: Photo Researchers, Inc.
58: Shirley Zeiberg Photography
60: Shirley Zeiberg Photography
63: Shirley Zeiberg Photography
64: Photo Researchers, Inc.
66: Shirley Zeiberg Photography
68: Shirley Zeiberg Photography
70: Shirley Zeiberg Photography
72: Shirley Zeiberg Photography
74: Shirley Zeiberg Photography
77: Shirley Zeiberg Photography
78: Shirley Zeiberg Photography
82: Shirley Zeiberg Photography
85: Shirley Zeiberg Photography
86: Shirley Zeiberg Photography

Senior Consulting Editor Carol C. Nadelson, M.D., is president and chief executive officer of the American Psychiatric Press, Inc., staff physician at Cambridge Hospital, and Clinical Professor of Psychiatry at Harvard Medical School. In addition to her work with the American Psychiatric Association, which she served as vice president in 1981-83 and president in 1985-86, Dr. Nadelson has been actively involved in other major psychiatric organizations, including the Group for the Advancement of Psychiatry, the American College of Psychiatrists, the Association for Academic Psychiatry, the American Association of Directors of Psychiatric Residency Training Programs, the American Psychosomatic Society, and the American College of Mental Health Administrators. In addition, she has been a consultant to the Psychiatric Education Branch of the National Institute of Mental Health and has served on the editorial boards of several journals. Doctor Nadelson has received many awards, including the Gold Medal Award for significant and ongoing contributions in the field of psychiatry, the Elizabeth Blackwell Award for contributions to the causes of women in medicine, and the Distinguished Service Award from the American College of Psychiatrists for outstanding achievements and leadership in the field of psychiatry.

Consulting Editor Claire E. Reinburg, M.A., is editorial director of the American Psychiatric Press, Inc., which publishes about 60 new books and six journals a year. She is a graduate of Georgetown University in Washington, D.C., where she earned bachelor of arts and master of arts degrees in English. She is a member of the Council of Biology Editors, the Women's National Book Association, the Society for Scholarly Publishing, and Washington Book Publishers.

As director of Write Stuff Editorial Service in New York City, **Elizabeth Russell Connolly** has written and edited for medical and business journals, trade magazines, high-tech firms, and various book publishers. She earned an MBA from New York University's Stern School in 1993 and a certificate in language studies from Freiburg Universitaet (Switzerland) in 1985. Her published work includes a global studies book for young adults; more than 14 Access travel guides covering North America, the Caribbean, and Europe; and several volumes in Chelsea House Publishers' Encyclopedia of Psychological Disorders.